# Unlock Your Potential:
## A Guide to Personal Growth for Job Seekers

First Edition,
Printed 2023, Houston, Texas
Copyright 2023
All Rights Reserved

**ISBN:** 9798861168366
**Imprint:** Independently published

# Contents

## About the Author

Hasina is a seasoned IT professional with 27 years of progressive IT experience and 13 years of working in alternative healthcare as a Classical Homeopath, Editor and Mentor.

Beginning her professional voyage, Hasina's initial foray into the technology landscape involved coding on early computing systems. As time progressed, her journey expanded to encompass innovative strides in software development, systems architecture, and the orchestration of mergers and integrations spanning various scales and contexts. She enjoys the challenge of seeing how older technologies can be updated and integrated into the newer technologies and still leave room for further enhancements in the future.

Beyond her IT accomplishments, Hasina's curiosity in the healthcare arena led her to embark on a comprehensive exploration of modern medical practices, culminating in her embrace of complementary medicines. Armed with training as a Classical Homeopath, she champions the cause of natural remedies, advocating for personal well-being through nutrition, relaxation strategies, and holistic healing agents.

Hasina also has an affinity in writing; to create works to inspire others and help them make positive changes in their lives.

Hasina finds solace in literary pursuits, artistic expression, coding, and mentoring others in their pursuits, embodying the equilibrium she ardently seeks to infuse into both her technological and healthcare journeys.

Amid a pivotal phase of career transitioning between jobs and in her career path, a notable realization dawned on her: the wealth of job-hunting resources available online and in literature did little to spare her from the laborious task of individually researching each aspect. The fragmented nature of information meant that a comprehensive resource was lacking. It was this very realization that spurred the creation of this book, driven by the sincere intention to alleviate the time and effort others invest in dissecting the intricate nuances of job hunting.

The creation of this book stems from the desire to enable individuals and alleviate the overwhelming nature of the job-hunting process, aiming to provide readers with a more enriching and productive experience—one that allows them to shift their focus solely on job hunting but to also lead them to discover more about themselves than they might have anticipated. The aspiration behind these pages is for readers to engage with the content and through the various exercises and examples offered, unravel their genuine passions and ambitions. Through this process, it's envisioned that individuals will unearth their true calling, matching their personality, passions, and expectations to a career that aligns harmoniously with them.

A note for those who have purchased this book, from the author....

# Good luck with your endeavors and wishing you land your perfect job. Don't ever give up on your dreams.

# Introduction

In the current dynamic, rapidly evolving and fiercely competitive job market, securing a job opportunity is no longer solely reliant on qualifications and experience nor does luck or chance come into play. Nowadays, it demands more from the candidate than ever before. It requires a proactive and strategic approach—one that encompasses personal growth and self-improvement. Welcome to "Unlock Your Potential: A Guide to Personal Growth for Job Seekers." In this transformative book, tailored specifically to job seekers like yourself, we will embark on a journey of self-discovery, empowerment, and actionable strategies that will propel you towards securing the job of your dreams. We'll explore the essential principles and actionable strategies that will empower you to stand out among other job seekers.

Chapter by chapter, we will delve into the essential principles and proven techniques that will equip you with the skills and mindset necessary to navigate the job search landscape with confidence and purpose. We understand that job seekers, whether recent graduates or seasoned professionals seeking a change, face unique challenges and uncertainties. That is why this book is designed to address those pain points head-on, providing you with the knowledge and resources needed to stand out from the competition and land that coveted position.

Throughout this guide, our aim is to empower you with actionable insights, practical exercises, and real-life examples that will resonate with your journey. We will not only help you discover your true potential but also provide you with the tools to communicate your unique value to potential employers effectively. We firmly believe that personal growth is the foundation upon which your career success can flourish, and we are committed to supporting you every step of the way.

It is necessary to explore the critical importance of understanding your unique value. By assessing your core skills, strengths, and passions, you will gain a deeper understanding of what sets you apart from other candidates. Through introspection and reflection, you will identify your transferable skills—those versatile abilities that can be applied to various roles and industries. We will guide you in uncovering your strengths, both hard and soft, and help you recognize the areas where you excel. Furthermore, we will encourage you to explore your passions and align them with potential career paths, fostering a sense of fulfillment and purpose.

Armed with this newfound self-awareness, we will move on to identifying your unique selling points (USPs). These are the qualities and attributes that differentiate you from other candidates in the job market. By defining your value proposition, you will gain clarity on how you can contribute to the success of an organization and solve their problems. Market research will play a pivotal role in this process, enabling you to stay informed about industry trends, emerging technologies, and employer expectations. Armed with this knowledge, you will craft a personal brand that authentically represents your unique qualities, aspirations, and expertise. A strong personal brand will distinguish you from the competition, attract the attention of employers, and open doors to exciting opportunities.

Building a personal brand is not limited to the virtual realm alone. In some circumstances, it will be necessary to develop a strong online presence and create a professional portfolio that showcases your skills and accomplishments. In many cases it would be beneficial to use the power of testimonials and recommendations to build credibility and trust with potential employers. By leveraging these strategies, you can position yourself as a sought-after candidate who is not only capable but also passionate and dedicated.

This book serves as a comprehensive guide, to help you to improve your resume writing skills, enhance your interview techniques, and provide in-depth guidance at every stage to demonstrate your commitment to potential employers. The transformative process outlined within these pages extends beyond the interview, supporting you in honing your skills and fostering a growth mindset that sets you apart from others.

Throughout this book, we will maintain a consistent structure, ensuring smooth transitions between chapters. Our writing style will be engaging, relatable, and easy to understand, prioritizing clarity over complexity. We aim to utilize formatting techniques, such as bold text and bullet points, to draw attention to essential points and provide a visually appealing reading experience. Additionally, we will incorporate compelling examples and real-life anecdotes to illustrate concepts and evoke emotions that resonate with your journey.

While the various chapters of this book may touch on overlapping concepts, it is important to note that these redundancies are intentional and serve a vital purpose. The intertwining of these concepts at each step reinforces their significance and underscores their importance in your journey. By revisiting and reinforcing these ideas, we emphasize their value and ensure a comprehensive understanding that will greatly benefit you in achieving your goals.

In each chapter, you will find actionable steps and exercises that encourage practical application. We firmly believe that personal growth is a continuous process, and by actively engaging with the material, you will be able to implement the strategies outlined in this book and witness tangible results.

It is important to acknowledge that this book was crafted using a range of tools, including state-of-the-art ChatGPT and AI tools, to enhance the language flow and coherence. Additionally, insights from industry leaders' personal experiences were incorporated to ensure the book's relevance to real-world situations.

Are you ready to embark on a transformative journey of personal growth and career advancement? Let's unlock your potential and set you on the path to finding a better job. In the following chapters, we will explore specific strategies, techniques, and insider tips that will equip you with the knowledge and confidence needed to navigate the job market successfully. Get ready to take charge of your future and unleash the best version of yourself.

Let's dive in.

# Chapter 1: Understanding Your Unique Value

In today's competitive job market, **standing out from the crowd is essential**. It's not enough to simply possess the required qualifications and experience. To truly shine and attract the attention of employers, you must understand and effectively communicate your unique value. In this chapter, we will embark on a journey of self-discovery, helping you assess your skills, strengths, and passions to unlock your distinct qualities that set you apart from other candidates.

## 1.1 Assessing Your Skills, Strengths, and Passions

To begin the process of self-evaluation, it is important to reflect on your skills and abilities. Consider the skills you have acquired through education, previous jobs, internships, or extracurricular activities to gain a better understanding of your strengths and possibly create a list of areas for further improvement. Be honest with your assessment. There is no right or wrong answer, only your answer, which will act as the guiding factor for all next steps of your personal journey.

Practical Exercise:

Using the following list of questions as a foundation, engage in self-reflection and self-assessment.

Construct your responses in the form of lists, avoiding lengthy written explanations. Each item in your lists will serve as a thought point or an entry on your resume. Focus on concise and impactful statements for each item.

Remember, the goal is to capture key information succinctly using bullet points or short phrases. These thought points will eventually serve as valuable entries on your resume and even on interviews, highlighting your achievements, skills, and experiences. Throughout the exercise, there may be redundancies and that's ok. The idea is to get as much down as possible during this reflection process.

An additional insight gained from this activity underscores the importance of regularly assessing your skill set, either annually or at significant milestones. By consistently updating your list of skills, you not only maintain an ongoing record but also begin to discern a discernible pattern in your professional development. This evolving catalog allows you to identify areas of strength, areas where skill enhancement and training might be beneficial, and whether you might be veering off course in pursuit of your goals, prompting a potential need to recalibrate your path.

Let's begin.

1. Identify your educational background. Outline your educational qualifications and any relevant certifications you have. List locations and dates next to each.

  - [Education 1]      - [Education 2]      - [Certification 1]      - [Certification 2]

2. What are your top five professional achievements or accomplishments in the last 5-10 years?

- [Achievement 1]   - [Achievement 2]   - [Achievement 3]   - [Achievement 4]   - [Achievement 5]

3. List your core skills and areas of expertise you currently have.

Evaluate areas where you excel and mark them, so you know what you need to highlight to prospective employers. Don't just rely on your professional skills. Think about what else you are good at. Where are your strengths and talents outside of your profession or studies?

Mark those skills that you consistently perform at a high level using one marker (ie. Use a star symbol). Mark those that you find most pleasurable to do with another marker (ie. Use two stars or a check symbol).

- [Skill 1]    - [Skill 2]    - [Skill 3]    - [Skill 4]    - [Skill 5]   - [Skill 6]

4. What activities have you participated in outside of formal education and work?

5. What roles or positions have you held throughout your career? In parenthesis next to each position, write down in short form what were your responsibilities and duties at these roles. List each as a separate skill you have acquired.

6. In your various roles, list any recognitions or notable results you received. These would be accomplishments or achievements that demonstrate the excellence you possess and can be readily shown to an employer.

7. What are your most significant contributions in your previous roles or projects? Reflect on tasks that come naturally to you. Which tasks or activities do you find easy to perform? What skills do you possess that make these tasks easier for you? What positive feedback or recognition have you received for these tasks? What skills or competencies did you gain from these activities? Make sure to quantify these situations so that it is tangible to the reader.

- [Contribution 1]    - [Contribution 2]    - [Contribution 3]

8. Identify your leadership experience and any notable achievements in leading teams. Did you hold any leadership positions or take on significant responsibilities that can be highlighted with details?

- [Leadership experience 1]   - [Leadership experience 2]
- [Notable achievement 1]     - [Notable achievement 2]

9. List your technical skills, software proficiencies, or specialized knowledge. What are your strengths and talents? In which areas do you consistently perform at a high level? What accomplishments or achievements demonstrate your excellence?

- [Technical skill 1]        - [Technical skill 2]
- [Software proficiency 1]        - [Software proficiency 2]
- [Specialized knowledge 1]        - [Specialized knowledge 2]

10. Reflect on your ability to adapt to change or handle challenging situations. Describe a situation where you had to make a quick decision and what were the results. Did you ever deal with a coworker or boss who you were not seeing eye to eye on something and what did you do? Make sure to list all such instances since each will show a different behavioral characteristic in handling challenging situations.

- [Ability to adapt to change 1]        - [Ability to adapt to change 2]
- [Handling challenging situations 1]    - [Handling challenging situations 2]

11. List any professional memberships, affiliations, or industry-related involvements.

- [Membership/Affiliation 1]        - [Membership/Affiliation 2]
- [Industry involvement 1]        - [Industry involvement 2]

12. Identify any additional languages you are proficient in, both written and spoken.

- [Language 1]    - [Language 2]      - [Language 3]

13. Reflect on your problem-solving and analytical skills.  Assess projects with remarkable results. Recall projects or initiatives where you achieved outstanding outcomes.  What specific skills or strategies contributed to those results?  How did you overcome challenges or obstacles during those projects?

- [Problem-solving skill 1]      - [Problem-solving skill 2]
- [Analytical skill 1]        - [Analytical skill 2]        - [Analytical skill 3]

> As you make note of your strengths and skills, also make note of anything you feel you would want to improve on and mark it with an asterisk or plus sign or something different from what you've been using thus far to highlight specific things.  You can use this list when we discuss developing your skills in a later chapter.

Real-Life Examples:

Top five professional achievements or accomplishments
- Led a successful product launch, resulting in a 30% increase in sales.
- Implemented a cost-saving initiative that resulted in annual savings of $100,000.
- Received recognition as "Employee of the Year" for exceptional performance and contributions.

- Migrated 23 physical servers to a virtual server thereby reducing server footprint in the lab by 60%
- Implemented a new warehouse from the ground up in Houston, increasing revenue by 12%.

Core skills and areas of expertise.
- Project management
- Data analysis
- Client relationship management

Most significant contributions in previous roles or projects?
- Developed and implemented a streamlined process that reduced project completion time by 20%.
- Led a cross-functional team to successfully deliver a complex project within budget and ahead of schedule.
- Implemented a customer feedback system, resulting in a 15% improvement in overall customer satisfaction.

Identify your leadership experience and any notable achievements in leading teams.
- Managed a team of 10 sales representatives, exceeding quarterly targets by 25%.
- Introduced a mentorship program, fostering professional growth and development within the team.
- Facilitated effective collaboration among team members, resulting in improved productivity and morale.
- Managed a team of 12 state-side employees in California, NY, NJ, Texas and Florida and 6 international employees based in India, Poland and Haiti.

Technical skills, software proficiencies, or specialized knowledge.
- Proficient in Microsoft Office Suite (Word, Excel, PowerPoint)
- Skilled in data visualization using Tableau
- Knowledgeable in programming languages such as C#, VB.NET, Python and SQL

Reflect on your ability to adapt to change or handle challenging situations.
- Quickly made a strategic decision during a crisis, mitigating potential risks and ensuring minimal disruption to operations.
- Successfully managed a project with constantly changing requirements and delivered it on time and within budget.
- Adapted to a new software system and trained colleagues on its implementation, enhancing overall team efficiency.

Describe a situation where you had to make a quick decision and outline the results.
- Made an on-the-spot decision to revise the marketing strategy, resulting in a 20% increase in customer engagement and sales.

Did you ever deal with a coworker or boss who you were not seeing eye to eye on something? What did you do?

> - Effectively communicated concerns and suggestions to find a compromise, resulting in a mutually beneficial outcome.
> - Actively sought feedback and engaged in open dialogue to bridge the communication gap and establish a productive working relationship.
> - Despite best efforts to improve employee's skills and communication capabilities, had to make the decision to let them go and find a better candidate for his position.

## References and Other Details

While you are jotting down your notes, this would be a good time to also make a list of personal references, job history, education and any other pertinent information that could be asked for on an application.

For references, reach out to people you know, who you've worked with, your previous bosses or teachers and ask them if it would be okay to put them down as references.  Make sure that they are willing to put in a good word for you and not just give a basic review.

Practical Exercise:

Create a list for each of the following and keep it at the ready for when filling out applications.

- Education – Include school, location, degree awarded, grade point average, honors, month and years attended.
- Work History – Include Company name, location, title, salary, month, and years worked, hours per week worked.  This would be a good place to include references from this company and separate them by company.
- Volunteer Work History
- References – Include Name, title, email, contact number, your relationship to them, month and years working with them.
- Memberships – Include name, level if applicable, years held.

## 1.1.1 Identify Transferable Skills

Start by identifying your **transferable skills, which are versatile abilities that can be applied to various roles and industries**. These skills include communication, problem-solving, leadership, teamwork, adaptability, and critical thinking. Reflect on specific instances where you have demonstrated these skills and how they have contributed to your success. Each transferable skill has qualities that will align with company objectives and goals, so it's essential to recognize where you have personally applied these skills.

*Communication* – Facilitated effective collaboration among team members, resulting in improved productivity and morale.

**Problem-solving** – Implemented a customer feedback system, resulting in a 15% improvement in overall customer satisfaction.

**Leadership** – Managed a team of 10 sales representatives, exceeding quarterly targets by 25%.

**Teamwork** – Led a cross-functional team to successfully deliver a complex project within budget and ahead of schedule.

**Adaptability** – Adapted to a new software system and trained colleagues on its implementation, enhancing overall team efficiency.

**Critical thinking** – Quickly made a strategic decision during a crisis, mitigating potential risks and ensuring minimal disruption to operations.

Practical Exercise with Example(s):
With the current list at your disposal, identify items that possess the characteristics of transferable skills defined above. If you come across additional instances that exemplify these transferable skills, add them to your running list. You can use a variety of markers, preferably in pastel or light hues, to accentuate the various skill categories. This approach will help you to quickly visualize your areas of strength, offering substantial guidance in pinpointing your true passions. Such insights can prove instrumental when faced with choices between different job opportunities and career paths.

When preparing for your interview, it is essential to consider these key transferable skills. Depending on the nature of the desired job, certain skills may hold more relevance than others. Therefore, it is advisable to prioritize and highlight those transferable skills that directly apply to the specific position you are seeking.

## 1.1.2 Uncover Your Strengths
Next, we need to **delve into your strengths**. These are the qualities that make you unique and exceptional. Consider both hard skills, such as technical expertise, and soft skills, such as empathy, creativity, or attention to detail. Reflect on situations where you have leveraged these strengths to achieve outstanding outcomes.

Think about the tasks that come naturally to you, the areas where you excel, and the projects where you have achieved remarkable results. These are the guiding factors in finding your strengths.

Practical Exercise:
From the list you have accumulated of your skills, take 5-10 skills that you have pertaining to the job and jot them down on a new list on a new page. This will point out those skills that you are very good at and would be able to talk about most freely and with confidence. These are the skills that you want to elaborate on in your resume and at an interview.

While you are doing this, review your running list and find 3-5 skills that you wish you could improve on for yourself. These skills are ones you possess some understanding of but require additional experience or training to develop a confident command over them. Depending on whether you want to build on them or not will define if it's a skill you would want to elaborate on in your resume or at an interview.

<u>Real-Life Examples:</u>
Skills I am good at:
- Patient during most situations.
- Very good at mathematical equations and problem solving.
- Technically proficient in many programming languages, servers, and tools.
- Work well under stress and through challenging situations.
- Network and Server administration
- Budgeting

Skills I wish I could improve:
- Budgeting skills and experiences related to it.
- Improve Python programming skills so that I can write better QA tests and automate testing.
- Increase knowledge of AWS and Azure services.

Don't forget to acknowledge your strengths and accomplishments while also being aware of your weaknesses. Take the time to evaluate the activities you enjoy doing and differentiate between the ones you excel at and the ones you may not be as proficient in. Recognize those things you really don't like to do or are poor at. These lists can help define the nature of the job you would excel at and those that you would be weak in.

### 1.1.3 Explore Your Passions

**Passions are the fuel that ignites a person's drive and enthusiasm.** They are the areas where you find fulfillment and enjoyment. Identify the subjects, topics, or activities that genuinely excite you. Think about how you can align your passions with potential career paths. Your passions provide the foundation for your soft skills, which you will bring to a job. Many companies consider this aspect to assess a candidate's compatibility with a particular position.

The following are some sites that can help you match some of your passions to job options.
- Jobtest.org
- Brainmanager.io
- mortenhansen.com

This site can help you analyze your behavior and habits: www.gallup.com.

Additional actions you can consider discovering how your passions can lead you to your dream job involve connecting with individuals in diverse fields that intrigue you and observing their career paths.

Practical Exercise with Example(s):

Create a table with two columns. In the first column list what you are passionate about. In the second column, next to each passion, try to put a possible career option that might meet your passions. You can search Job listings and job sites to find possible job options and names.

Avoid confining yourself solely to your existing knowledge base.

Extend your exploration beyond established boundaries and discover what the world has to offer that aligns with your passions. This is where your capacity for creative thinking becomes invaluable; make full use of it.

| Passion | Possible Career(s) |
| --- | --- |
| Walking in parks; working with nature, plants. | Forest Ranger, Parks Maintenance, Botanist |
| Programming in C# | IT Engineer |
| Homeopathic Teachings, IT | Website Builder, Scientist, Naturopath, Teacher |
| Designing applications | Software Engineer, Manager |
| Health and wellness | Healthcare, Nutritionist, Fitness Trainer, Health Coach |
| Social justice | Policeman, Lawyer, Judge, HR Admin |
| Painting | Graphic designer, Advertising, Filmmaking, Photographer |
| Managing people and projects | Project Manager, Systems Analyst, HR Admin, Executive level jobs, Coach, Teacher |

By exploring industries and professions that resonate with your passions, you can find fulfillment and enjoyment in your work while making a meaningful impact in areas that genuinely excite you.

## 1.2 Identifying Your Unique Selling Points- USPs

Once you have a clearer understanding of your skills, strengths, and passions, you will need to identify your **unique selling points** (USPs). These are the qualities and attributes that differentiate you from other candidates. USPs enable you to craft a personal brand that resonates with employers and showcases your value proposition.

In addition to the basic technical skills required by the position, you should make every effort to remember to mention all six selling points using real and tangible examples: Leadership, Problem-solving, Communication, Adaptable, Cross-cultural Competence and Innovative.

Practical Exercise
1. *Sell your Leadership Abilities*:
   - Highlight your track record of successfully leading teams or projects, demonstrating your ability to inspire and motivate others towards achieving goals.

- Emphasize your strong decision-making skills, strategic thinking, and the ability to take initiative, setting you apart as a natural leader among other candidates.

2. *Sell your Problem-Solving Skills:*
- Showcase your aptitude for identifying and resolving complex problems, showcasing your analytical thinking, creativity, and adaptability.
- Provide examples of situations where you effectively analyzed challenges, developed innovative solutions, and achieved successful outcomes, distinguishing you as a problem solver.

3. *Sell your Communication and Interpersonal Skills:*
- Illustrate your exceptional communication skills, both verbal and written, along with your ability to engage and connect with diverse individuals or audiences.
- Highlight your active listening, empathy, and negotiation skills, demonstrating your capacity to foster positive relationships and collaborate effectively with others.

4. *Sell your Technical Proficiency:*
- Highlight your advanced technical expertise, such as programming languages, software proficiency, or specialized knowledge relevant to the position you are applying for.
- Discuss how your technical skills enable you to contribute to projects, streamline processes, or introduce innovative solutions, positioning you as a valuable asset.

5. *Sell your Adaptability and Resilience to Changing Conditions and Situations:*
- Share examples of situations where you successfully adapted to change, overcame obstacles, or thrived in dynamic environments.
- Emphasize your ability to remain calm under pressure, embrace challenges, and quickly adapt to new circumstances, making you a resilient candidate.

6. *Sell your Cross-Cultural Competency with Diverse Teams:*
- Highlight your experiences and skills in navigating diverse cultural environments, demonstrating your ability to work effectively with individuals from different backgrounds.
- Showcase your understanding and appreciation of cultural nuances, adaptability to different working styles, and ability to foster inclusive and collaborative environments.

7. *Sell your Innovativeness and Creativity:*
- Discuss your ability to think outside the box, generate unique ideas, and contribute innovative solutions to problems.
- Share examples of instances where your creative thinking led to novel approaches, improved processes, or enhanced outcomes, showcasing your value as a creative thinker.

Your goal is to get the following selling point across to the hiring manager:

**I am an Innovative and Resilient Problem-solving Leader who can Communicate well with Diverse teams.**

### 1.2.1 Define Your Value Proposition

Consider what makes you special and what you can bring to an organization. Your value proposition should align with the needs and expectations of employers.

Ask yourself the following questions:
- What problems can I solve for employers?
- How can I contribute to the success of a company?
- What unique perspective or expertise do I offer?
- What job criteria are there that I can meet or go beyond 100%?

> The best way to find VPs is to first peruse the job description and then capture those skills that you can personally convey using your experience and education.

Remember, the examples provided so far serve as starting points to identify your unique selling points and value propositions. Reflect on your own experiences, skills, and achievements to determine the qualities and attributes that set you apart from other candidates and meet the job requirements.

Craft a personal brand that effectively communicates your value proposition to employers, showcasing the specific ways you can contribute to their organization's success.

### 1.2.2 Conduct Market Research

It is highly advisable to conduct thorough research on the job market and industries that pique your interest at this stage. Explore various job sites to review the available positions and the desired skill sets employers are seeking. Identify the skills and qualities you possess that are most valued by employers.

After meeting the essential criteria, pay attention to trends, emerging technologies, or industry-specific requirements that can augment your value proposition. Seek opportunities to enhance your skill set and align it with the evolving needs of the industry.

> It is always important to stay informed about the latest developments in your profession and adapt your skills accordingly.

### 1.2.3 Craft Your Personal Brand

**Your personal brand is the image and reputation you cultivate in the professional world.** It should reflect your unique qualities, values, and aspirations. Create a concise and compelling personal brand statement that communicates your USPs and resonates with your target audience. Craft a captivating elevator pitch that showcases your strengths, experiences, and career goals.

Practical Exercise:
Now is a good moment to review what you have so far and create an inventory of all your skills, without duplication.
- Compile a **comprehensive list** of the skills you have identified through self-reflection.
- Categorize them based on their relevance to the unique selling points we've discussed so far.
    - *Leadership, Problem-solving, Communication, Adaptable, Cross-cultural Competence and Innovative*
- Rank each of your skills based on your confidence level and proficiency in each. (For example, 5 being highly confident and 1 being very little confidence)
- Next to each skill, mark those skills that you have a passion for with a plus sign. These are the skills you want to be able to speak of very confidently at an interview.
- Highlight those that fall into the six transferable skills.
    - *communication, problem-solving, leadership, teamwork, adaptability, and critical thinking*


## 1.3 Building a Personal Brand That Stands Out

Now that you have a clear understanding of your skills, strengths, passions, and USPs, it's time to build a personal brand that captivates employers and sets you apart from the competition.

### 1.3.1 Develop a Strong Online Presence

In today's digital age, your online presence plays a crucial role in shaping your personal brand. Optimize your LinkedIn profile to showcase your skills, experiences, and achievements. Share relevant articles, insights, or projects that highlight your expertise. Engage in professional communities and discussions to expand your network.

Maintain brevity in all your interactions. Practice honesty and adhere to the essential messages you intend to convey. If your content appears insincere or lacks relevance, readers may quickly move on to other candidates.

Real-Life Example:
Here are some ways on how you can optimize your LinkedIn profile to effectively showcase your skills, experiences, and achievements, while actively engaging in professional communities.

1. *Profile Optimization:*
    - Craft a compelling headline that highlights your expertise, industry, and value proposition.
    - Write a concise and engaging summary that provides an overview of your background, skills, and accomplishments.
    - Incorporate relevant keywords throughout your profile to enhance searchability and increase visibility.

- Showcase your professional experiences, focusing on achievements, responsibilities, and quantifiable results.
- Include a professional headshot and ensure that your profile is complete and up to date.

2. *Skills and Endorsements:*
   - Identify and prioritize the key skills that align with your professional goals and target industries.
   - Request endorsements from colleagues, supervisors, or clients who can vouch for your proficiency in those skills.
   - Regularly review and update your skills section to reflect your current areas of expertise.

3. *Engaging Content:*
   - Share articles, blog posts, or industry insights that are relevant to your field and demonstrate your knowledge.
   - Create or contribute to meaningful discussions in professional groups on LinkedIn to showcase your expertise and engage with industry peers.
   - Share your own projects, case studies, or notable accomplishments to provide tangible evidence of your capabilities.
   - Utilize media elements such as videos, infographics, or presentations to enhance the visual appeal and engagement of your profile.

4. *Professional Networking:*
   - Actively connect with professionals in your industry, including colleagues, alumni, industry leaders, and potential mentors.
   - Personalize connection requests to establish rapport and express genuine interest in networking.
   - Engage with your connections by commenting on their posts, sharing valuable insights, or offering support.
   - Participate in industry-related discussions, webinars, or virtual events to expand your network and build relationships.

5. *Recommendations and Testimonials:*
   - Request recommendations from colleagues, supervisors, or clients who can provide positive testimonials about your work ethic, skills, and contributions.
   - Display these recommendations prominently on your profile to add credibility and reinforce your professional reputation.

6. *Continuous Learning:*
   - Showcase your commitment to professional development by highlighting relevant courses, certifications, or webinars you have completed.
   - Engage in continuous learning and stay updated on industry trends, sharing your insights and experiences with your network.

By implementing these strategies, you can optimize your LinkedIn profile to create a compelling personal brand, position yourself as an industry expert, and expand your professional network within your field of interest.

When engaging on other social media platforms, make an effort to maintain a semblance of normalcy in your personal updates unrelated to your career aspirations. Steer clear of excessive political activism, offensive conduct, or the use of harsh language. These behaviors can be perceived negatively and potentially influence how a potential employer or colleague perceives you. In the present landscape, employers do take into account a candidate's presence on various media platforms and may use it as an additional factor in their evaluation process.

> Don't be afraid to make use of tools like ChatGPT to enhance the visual and verbal aspects of each description and summary you incorporate on LinkedIn. These tools can help you to prepare a polished and professional image for yourself to effectively showcase your skills and experiences.
>
> Furthermore, allocate a portion of your time to peruse LinkedIn profiles of other individuals who have embraced similar career paths and choices as yours. Evaluate the potential of incorporating elements from their summaries to enhance your own. However, make sure that you avoid plagiarism by striving for originality. Use your own words to effectively underscore your skills and strengths.

### 1.3.2 Create a Professional Portfolio

A professional portfolio is a powerful tool to demonstrate your skills and accomplishments. Include samples of your work, projects, or presentations that showcase your expertise. Tailor your portfolio to align with the industries or roles you are targeting. Consider creating a personal website to house your portfolio and provide additional information about your skills and experiences.

Starting the process of building a portfolio might appear dauting and intimidating at first, but numerous platforms are available to assist you in taking the first steps. Utilizing educational resources like YouTube, Udemy, WordPress, GoDaddy, and similar platforms, you can swiftly acquire the skills needed to create your own portfolio.

Keep in mind that a portfolio can be as straightforward as a website featuring links to your previous work, articles you've authored, and a comprehensive list showcasing your skills and passions. **It serves as a dynamic representation of your accomplishments and expertise**.

Real-Life Example:
Here are some examples for Building a Professional Portfolio for various professions.

*Graphic Designer:*
- Include a variety of design samples such as logos, brochures, website mock-ups, or infographics that highlight your creativity and proficiency in design software.
- Showcase before-and-after examples to demonstrate your ability to enhance visuals and communicate visually appealing messages.
- Consider creating a personal website that showcases your portfolio and provides insights into your design process and client testimonials.

*Software Developer:*
- Showcase projects you have worked on, including code snippets, websites, mobile applications, or software prototypes that highlight your programming skills and problem-solving abilities.
- Include descriptions of your role, the technologies used, and any notable features or challenges overcome in each project.
- Consider including a link to your GitHub or other version control platforms to provide additional evidence of your coding expertise.

*Content Writer:*
- Feature writing samples that demonstrate your versatility and expertise in various formats, such as blog posts, articles, whitepapers, or social media content.
- Highlight your ability to write for different target audiences and industries by including samples from various niches or sectors.
- Consider creating a personal blog as part of your portfolio to showcase your writing skills, share your thoughts on industry-related topics, and engage with your audience.

*Marketing Strategist:*
- Include examples of marketing campaigns you have developed, including campaign briefs, content calendars, social media posts, email newsletters, or advertising materials.
- Highlight your ability to craft compelling marketing messages and create engaging content that drives results.
- Consider including case studies that demonstrate the impact of your strategies and the measurable outcomes achieved.

*Photographer:*
- Showcase a diverse range of your best photography work, categorized by genres such as portraits, landscapes, events, or product photography.
- Include high-quality images that demonstrate your technical skills, composition, and ability to capture moments effectively.
- Consider creating a visually appealing website or online gallery to showcase your photography portfolio and provide contact information for potential clients.

*Project Manager:*
- Create a personal website where you can provide insights into your project management approach, methodologies used, and highlight your career achievements.

- Include a few project artifacts such as project plans, Gantt charts, risk registers, and status reports to demonstrate your proficiency in project management methodologies and tools.
- Provide a section on your website that showcases your certifications or training in project management, such as PMP.

Remember that your professional portfolio should be tailored to the industries or roles you are targeting. It should showcase your skills, expertise, and accomplishments effectively. Including a personal website as a central hub for your portfolio provides an opportunity to showcase additional information about your skills, experiences, and contact details, enhancing your online presence and professional brand.

### 1.3.3 Leverage Testimonials and Recommendations
Testimonials and recommendations from colleagues, supervisors, or mentors can add credibility to your personal brand. Reach out to individuals who have worked closely with you and request testimonials that highlight your strengths, work ethic, and professionalism. Display these testimonials strategically on your personal website or LinkedIn profile.

Practical Exercise:
Work with people you know to get a few reviews added on your LinkedIn profile section.
- Reach out to three individuals from your professional network and kindly request them to provide a review or testimonial on your LinkedIn profile. Ask them if they could mention the following skills: leadership, communication, problem solving, technical capabilities, creativity, people management and adaptability.
- Reach out to one to two people in your friend's circle, outside of your profession, to write a review on LinkedIn describing your personality and ability to work with diverse groups of people.

### 1.4 The Elevator Pitch
At this point, while you have a list of all your skills readily available, it is important to know that crafting a compelling elevator pitch is key to making a memorable impression during the interviewing process. A concise and engaging pitch will effectively communicate your skills, experiences, and career aspirations in a short time. Once you have one elevator pitch, you can tailor your pitch to different contexts, whether it's a formal networking event or an impromptu meeting.

Here are some key points to consider when crafting an elevator pitch.

1. **Conciseness:**
   Keep your pitch brief and to the point. Aim for a duration of around 30 seconds to one minute, capturing the listener's attention without overwhelming them with excessive information.

## 2. Clarity:

Clearly communicate who you are, what you do, and the value you bring. Use simple and jargon-free language that can be easily understood by anyone, regardless of their industry or background.

## 3. Unique Selling Proposition:

Highlight your unique skills, experiences, or qualities that set you apart from others. Focus on what makes you special and the value you can offer to potential employers, clients, or collaborators.

## 4. Audience Relevance:

Tailor your pitch to the specific audience or context. Customize the message based on the needs and interests of the listener. Show how your skills or expertise can address their pain points or contribute to their goals.

## 5. Engaging Hook:

Start your pitch with a captivating hook that grabs attention and generates curiosity. A compelling opening statement can make the listener eager to learn more about you and your work.

## 6. Examples or Results:

Incorporate brief examples or tangible results to support your claims. Share specific accomplishments or projects that showcase your skills and illustrate the impact you can make.

## 7. Practice and Delivery:

Rehearse your elevator pitch to ensure a smooth and confident delivery. Pay attention to your tone, pace, and body language to convey enthusiasm and professionalism. Aim for a conversational tone rather than sounding rehearsed or robotic.

## 8. Call to Action:

End your pitch with a clear call to action. Depending on the context, it could be requesting a follow-up meeting, exchanging contact information, or exploring potential collaboration. Encourage the listener to take the next step in engaging with you.

Remember, **an elevator pitch is a versatile tool that can be adapted to various situations, such as networking events, job interviews, or professional introductions**. Continually refine and tailor your elevator pitch based on feedback, practice, and the specific objectives you want to achieve.

> By utilizing ChatGPT, you can input key bullet points from your resume or skillset and request a polished and succinct elevator pitch. Incorporating tools that enhance your user experience and aid in self-improvement poses no harm and can be highly beneficial.

Practical Exercise:

Ask ChatGPT: Given my extensive professional skills here {INSERT LIST OF QUALIFICATIONS}, please create an elevator pitch. <enter>

ChatGPT Result: Certainly! Based on your extensive experience, here's an elevator pitch example:

> "I am a highly skilled and versatile IT professional with a proven track record in managing diverse projects, teams, and IT infrastructure. With a strong background in managing personnel, budgets, and vendor relationships, I have successfully implemented numerous initiatives that have streamlined operations, enhanced security, and optimized productivity. From legacy system migrations and cloud-based technology integration to EDI retail solutions and web application development, I bring expertise in a wide range of technologies and platforms. I am known for my ability to navigate complex requirements, foster collaboration, and drive results. My passion for continuous improvement, combined with my strong leadership and communication skills, have consistently delivered outstanding outcomes. I am seeking new opportunities where I can leverage my expertise and contribute to the success of innovative organizations."

Remember that if this seems too long, you can ask ChatGPT to shorten it further.

Ask ChatGPT: Given this elevator pitch {INSERT THE SUMMARY ABOVE}, make it shorter and concise.

ChatGPT Result:

> I'm an adept IT professional with a proven record in project management, team leadership, and IT infrastructure. My background in personnel management, budgeting, and vendor relations has fueled successful initiatives, optimizing operations, bolstering security, and elevating productivity. With expertise spanning legacy migrations, cloud integration, EDI solutions, and web apps, I excel in diverse technologies. I'm recognized for navigating complexities, fostering collaboration, and achieving results. Equipped with strong leadership and communication skills, I drive continuous improvement. I'm eager to apply my expertise to innovative organizations.

If this still seems too wordy, you can practice it by breaking it down into a few short list items. This can help you to use your own words and still highlight the key points.

> I'm an IT professional with a proven record in project management, team leadership, and IT infrastructure.

I have a background in
- Software development,
- personnel management,
- budgeting,
- and vendor relations

I have had success in many of my initiatives.
- optimizing operations,
- bolstering security,
- elevating productivity
- migrating legacy systems,
- cloud integration,
- EDI solutions,
- and web applications.

I excel in diverse technologies in development, day to day operations and in management. I'm recognized for
- navigating complexities,
- fostering collaboration,
- and achieving results.

I have strong leadership and communication skills and a drive for continuous improvement. I'm eager to apply my expertise to innovative organizations.

Ultimately, **your elevator pitch will need to highlight your key skills, experiences, and accomplishments, while showcasing your adaptability, leadership abilities, and technical prowess in a few short sentences**. Tailor and refine your pitch based on the specific context and audience you are addressing.

## 1.5 Conclusion

By understanding your unique value, identifying your Unique Selling Points (USPs), and establishing a distinctive personal brand, you will position yourself as a highly sought-after candidate in the job market. Employers will be naturally drawn to your exceptional qualities and recognize the significant value you can bring to their organization.

It's important to bear in mind that potential employers are in search of individuals who can wholeheartedly contribute to the company's mission and objectives. They seek candidates who exude confidence in their skillset and can openly express their thoughts and passions without hesitation. It's very important that you believe in yourself and in your capabilities. If there is any doubt, then review your list again and again until you realize your potential to achieve your goals with unwavering confidence.

This chapter has ideally equipped you with the tools and insights necessary to embark on a journey of self-discovery and present your most compelling self to the professional world. Utilize the exercises to compile a comprehensive list that accentuates your remarkable skills, enabling you to progress to the next stages of your job search.

# Chapter 2: Goal Setting for Career Success

Welcome to Chapter 2 of our book on personal growth and career success. In this chapter, we will dive into the critical process of goal setting and how it can help you pave the path to finding a better job. By setting clear and actionable goals, you can create a roadmap for success and stay motivated throughout your career journey. Let's explore the art of setting SMART goals, creating an effective action plan, and overcoming obstacles to achieve your aspirations.

## 2.1 Understanding SMART Goals

Setting goals is not just about dreaming big; it's about creating a roadmap that leads to tangible results.

SMART goals provide a framework to ensure your goals are **Specific, Measurable, Achievable, Relevant, and Time-bound**.

Let's break down each element so you can apply it to yourself and your objectives.

1. **Specific**:

   Clearly define your goals to give them clarity and direction. For example, instead of saying, "I want a better job," be specific and say, "I want to secure a managerial position in a reputable marketing firm within the next two years."

2. **Measurable**:

   Establish criteria to track your progress and measure your success. This could be quantifiable metrics such as the number of job applications submitted, the number of interviews attended, or the percentage increase in salary.

3. **Achievable**:

   Set goals that are realistic and within your reach. While it's important to dream big, setting unattainable goals can lead to frustration and disappointment. Consider your current skills, qualifications, and resources to ensure your goals are achievable.

4. **Relevant**:

   Align your goals with your long-term career aspirations and personal values. Ensure they are meaningful and relevant to your desired career path. For example, if your goal is to work in a creative field, pursuing a position that allows you to utilize your artistic talents would be relevant.

5. **Time-bound**:

   Set a deadline for achieving your goals. This helps create a sense of urgency and keeps you focused. Breaking down your goals into smaller, time-bound milestones can also help you stay motivated and track your progress along the way.

Practical Exercise:

Work on your SMART list using the final list you created in Chapter 1.

## 2.2 Creating an Action Plan to Achieve Your Goals

Once you have defined your SMART goals, it's time to create an action plan that will guide you towards their attainment. An action plan helps break down your goals into actionable steps and provides a roadmap for success.

Here are some ways on how you can create an effective action plan to reach your SMART goals.

1. **Identify key milestones:**

   Divide your goal into smaller milestones or tasks that need to be accomplished along the way. For example, if your goal is to land a job in a specific industry, your milestones could include updating your resume, networking with professionals in the field, and attending industry-related events.

2. **Prioritize tasks:**

   Determine the order in which you need to complete your tasks. Identify which tasks are time-sensitive or have dependencies on other tasks. This helps you stay organized and ensures you focus on the most important actions first.

3. **Set deadlines:**

   Assign deadlines to each task or milestone in your action plan. This creates a sense of urgency and helps you stay accountable to your goals. Be realistic when setting deadlines, considering your other commitments and the complexity of the tasks.

4. **Allocate resources:**

   Identify the resources you need to accomplish each task. This could include time, money, access to professional development opportunities, or support from mentors or coaches. Ensure you have the necessary resources to execute your action plan effectively.

5. **Monitor and adjust:**

   Regularly review and assess your progress. Track your accomplishments, make adjustments to your plan as needed, and celebrate your milestones along the way. Stay adaptable and open to changes, as your career journey may present unexpected opportunities or challenges.

Practical Exercise:

Based on your exploration of career goals, identify potential courses that align with your goals. Look for options that are both cost-effective and offer relatively swift certification or completion timelines. This approach allows you to attain certification with foundational knowledge while also demonstrating to potential employers your steadfast commitment to realizing your career ambitions.

Once you've identified the courses you intend to take, arrange them in order of priority and incorporate them into your schedule. It's crucial to remain diligent and prevent them from slipping off your radar. Stay dedicated to these courses and pursue the certifications they offer, if applicable. The sooner you accomplish this, the quicker you can leverage them to showcase your competencies.

Regularly assess your advancement and make necessary adjustments to your schedules to ensure the successful completion of each course.

Upon finishing each course, proactively update your LinkedIn profile and resume with the pertinent details.

Many individuals find themselves balancing responsibilities within their families, careers, and personal lives. It's common for time to be in short supply or so tightly scheduled that it may seem impossible to carve out any moments for self-improvement. However, adopting such an attitude during your job search is not the most productive approach.

At this juncture, it's crucial to seek out motivation that propels you to allocate even just half an hour to learning, as this investment will significantly contribute to your future development. This motivation could stem from the desire for a better job, increased compensation, or even personal satisfaction. In essence, **finding that sliver of time can become a pivotal step toward achieving your professional aspirations**.

## 2.3 Overcoming Obstacles and Staying Motivated

Achieving your goals is not always a smooth journey. Obstacles and setbacks are inevitable, but with the right mindset and strategies, you can overcome them and stay motivated. Here are some tips to help you overcome obstacles and maintain your drive.

1. **Embrace a growth mindset:**
   View obstacles as opportunities for growth and learning. Embrace challenges as steppingstones toward your goals. Cultivate a positive attitude and believe in your ability to overcome obstacles.

2. **Seek support:**
   Surround yourself with a network of supportive individuals who can offer guidance, advice, and encouragement. Seek out mentors, join professional communities, and leverage online resources to gain insights and support.

3. **Break it down:**
   If you encounter a particularly daunting obstacle, break it down into smaller, manageable steps. This makes it easier to tackle and gives you a sense of progress along the way.

4. **Stay focused on the WHY:**
   Remind yourself of why you set these goals in the first place. Reflect on your passions, values, and long-term aspirations. Keeping your purpose at the forefront of your mind will fuel your motivation and help you push through challenges.

**5. Celebrate milestones:**

>Celebrate your achievements, no matter how small. Acknowledge your progress and reward yourself for the effort and dedication you put into reaching your goals. This reinforces positive behavior and keeps you motivated for the next phase of your career journey.

## 2.4 Conclusion:

Setting SMART goals, creating an action plan, and overcoming obstacles are essential components of achieving career success. By implementing the strategies outlined in this chapter, you are well on your way to finding a better job and realizing your full potential. Remember, goal setting is an ongoing process, so regularly review and adjust your goals as your career evolves. Stay motivated, stay focused, and never stop striving for personal and professional growth.

# Chapter 3: Crafting an Effective Job Search Strategy

Crafting an effective job search strategy is crucial for maximizing your chances of finding the right job in the right market.    At this point, you will have conducted a thorough self-assessment to identify your core skills, strengths, and areas of expertise.  You will have defined your career goals and aspirations. You've reflected on your long-term objectives, defined a preferred industry, and desired job role. You might even have identified one or more specific companies or sectors you wish to work in.

**Having this clear direction will help guide your job search efforts and narrow down your efforts to meaningful searches**.

## 3.1 Researching Industries and Companies for Job Leads

It is time to research the job market and look for potential employers. Explore the job market to gain insights into current trends, in-demand skills, and job opportunities. Identify the industries and companies that are actively hiring in your desired field. Stay updated on industry news, emerging technologies, and market conditions that may impact job prospects.

Identify those companies that align with your career goals and values. Research their mission, culture, recent news, and employee experiences. Follow the company on social media, sign up for their newsletters, and monitor their career pages for job openings. Tailor your applications to match each company's values and requirements. By targeting specific companies and showing that you have done some research, you are showing your interest in working with them and their goals.

Observe that while the paragraphs above may appear to be summaries, it is imperative to dissect them into separate points and thoroughly evaluate each one for its worth. In your job search, remember not to neglect the crucial aspect of researching companies; their identity and values are equally significant.

### 3.1.1 Company Sites

A significant number of employers choose to exclusively post job openings on their own dedicated career websites, encouraging potential candidates to utilize these platforms for their job searches. If you have specific companies in mind where you aspire to work, commencing your search on their official sites can be a strategic approach.

Dedicating time to explore both private sector job opportunities and governmental job portals is equally crucial. Public sector jobs often provide stable career prospects, comprehensive benefits, and a diverse range of roles. By exploring government job sites, you can uncover openings in areas you might not have initially considered.

### 3.1.2 Network Contacts

Harness the benefits of tapping into your personal network, which encompasses family members, friends, current and former coworkers, professional acquaintances, and past colleagues. Take the initiative to inform them of your ongoing job search, expressing your earnest desire for their backing and assistance in unearthing promising job opportunities. By actively engaging with your network, you not only showcase your dedication but also open the doors to potential referrals and leads. Initiating conversations and inquiring about potential job openings or introductions can yield unexpected yet immensely beneficial results. Your network might have insights into unadvertised positions, companies with imminent hiring needs, or can connect you with individuals who might be influential in your chosen field.

Moreover, consider actively participating in networking events, industry conferences, and virtual meetups that pertain to your area of interest. These gatherings offer fertile ground for expanding your professional connections and forging valuable relationships. They provide a platform for sharing experiences, insights, and industry knowledge, potentially leading to opportunities that might not have otherwise crossed your path.

For instance, attending an industry-specific conference can lead to encounters with professionals from diverse backgrounds who can introduce you to companies looking for candidates with your skill set. Similarly, joining virtual meetups related to your field can connect you with like-minded individuals and even potential employers seeking talents like yours.

The power of networking lies in the potential for genuine, human connections to pave the way for unforeseen career breakthroughs. Embrace these opportunities to forge bonds that can extend beyond your job search, potentially influencing your professional journey for years to come.

Here are some sites that cater to helping individuals find jobs.
> https://www.linkedin.com/company/tealhq/
> https://www.linkedin.com/company/swoopednetwork/
> https://www.linkedin.com/company/working-nomads/
> https://www.linkedin.com/company/we-work-remotely/
> https://www.linkedin.com/company/flexjobs-com/
> https://www.linkedin.com/company/justremote/
> https://www.linkedin.com/company/dynamite-jobs/


### 3.1.3 Job Search Aggregators

If you are uncertain about which companies align with your professional aspirations, turning to job boards becomes a valuable strategy. These platforms aggregate job postings from diverse industries, streamlining the process and granting you access to a wide array of promising opportunities. For instance, if you're a software engineer, job boards can unveil openings in tech startups, established tech giants, and even non-tech companies looking for in-house tech expertise.

Exploring job boards is particularly advantageous when you're in the exploration phase of your job search or looking to broaden your horizons across various sectors. It offers a comprehensive overview of the job landscape, showcasing options you might not have otherwise considered.

Explore the possibility of leveraging well-regarded job search platforms and aggregators, such as LinkedIn, Indeed, SimplyHired, Glassdoor, FlexJobs, FindIt (formerly Monster), LinkUp, and specialized industry-specific job boards, to unearth a wealth of job openings.

Employ the advanced filtering options that these platforms provide to meticulously tailor your search criteria, enhancing the precision of your job hunt. Additionally, consider setting up email notifications that promptly alert you to new job postings that match your preferences.

These platforms offer not only convenience but also insights into the job market, industry trends, and company cultures through reviews and ratings. Engage with these platforms proactively to amplify your job search effectiveness, staying attuned to evolving opportunities that align with your aspirations.

### 3.1.4 Other Sources

It's advisable to consider subscribing to professional journals that frequently feature mentions of companies within your field. Beyond company news, these journals often encompass a wealth of valuable insights, industry trends, and relevant analyses. Moreover, such publications might offer a platform for job listings that originate from diverse sources, giving you a broader perspective on available opportunities.

These journals can serve as a means to stay updated with the latest happenings in your industry, understand the challenges and innovations companies are facing, and potentially uncover hidden opportunities. By immersing yourself in the content of these journals, you can deepen your industry knowledge and gain a competitive edge in your job search.

As you explore these journals, pay attention not only to the job listings but also to the narratives and profiles of professionals who have made significant contributions in your field. These stories can provide valuable insights into career trajectories and strategies for success.

Incorporating the information gleaned from these journals into your job search and networking efforts can foster a well-rounded approach to advancing your career.

Consider engaging with headhunters and professionals who specialize in assisting individuals in their job search and placement. Prepare to engage in conversations about your career objectives, your proficiencies across different domains, and be open to flexibility regarding potential job options. Sometimes, the job you secure, even if it deviates from your initial expectations, may turn out to be the ideal opportunity you had been wanting all along.

Real-Life Example:

Log onto several different job sites and set up job alerts. Customize your search criteria to receive notifications for relevant positions only or you will be bombarded with too many to investigate.

Regularly monitor these platforms for new job postings.

Based on your career goals and market research, refine your job search criteria as much as you can. Consider factors such as location, industry, job title, company size, and salary range. This will help you focus your efforts on opportunities that align with your preferences.

### 3.1.4 Virtual Job Fairs and Recruiting Events

Many states, schools, and businesses provide virtual and in-person job fairs, career expos, and industry-specific events. Keep a lookout for these types of events and try to attend those that interest you the most. These events also provide opportunities to connect with recruiters, learn about job openings, and showcase your skills and qualifications.

Make sure to prepare your elevator pitch and have copies of your resume on hand, so you can make a positive impression from the get-go.

In addition to traditional job fairs, virtual job fairs and recruiting events have become increasingly common. These online events allow you to interact with recruiters, attend presentations, and apply for job opportunities. Research upcoming virtual events in your industry and register to connect with potential employers and explore job openings.

### 3.1.5 Mobile Apps

Download job search mobile apps like Indeed, LinkedIn, or Glassdoor to access job opportunities on the go. These apps often offer features like personalized job recommendations, job alerts, and the ability to apply for jobs directly from your mobile device.

### 3.2 Staying Organized

Staying organized throughout your job search is crucial for effective progress tracking and timely follow-ups. By maintaining a record of the jobs you've applied for, important deadlines, and any feedback received, you can enhance your efficiency and increase your chances of success.

Here are some key aspects to consider when staying organized.

1. **Job application tracker:**
   Create a spreadsheet or use a job search platform to keep track of the jobs you have applied to. Include details such as the company name, position title, application date, and any other relevant information. This tracker will help you have a clear overview of your applications and ensure that you follow up appropriately.

2. **Important deadlines:**

Take note of application deadlines, interview dates, or any other time-sensitive information related to each job opportunity. Having a centralized place to record these deadlines will ensure that you never miss an important date and can proactively follow up as needed.

3. **Follow-up schedule:**

Establish a follow-up schedule to remind yourself when to check in with employers after submitting an application or completing an interview. This can include sending a follow-up email or making a phone call to inquire about the status of your application. By staying organized with your follow-ups, you demonstrate your continued interest and professionalism.

4. **Feedback and notes:**

Keep a record of any feedback or notes received during the application process or interviews. This can include comments on your resume, interview performance, or areas of improvement. By documenting this feedback, you can reflect on it and make necessary adjustments for future applications or interviews.

5. **Document management:**

Organize your documents related to each job application, such as tailored resumes, cover letters, or portfolios. Maintain a system, either physical or digital, to easily retrieve the required documents when needed. This helps streamline the application process and ensures that you have everything readily available.

6. **Online tools and apps:**

Utilize job search and organizational tools or apps that are designed to assist in tracking applications, deadlines, and follow-ups. These tools can provide automated reminders, store relevant information, and help you stay on top of your job search activities.

By staying organized throughout your job search, you maintain a structured approach and avoid missing crucial opportunities. It enables you to efficiently manage your progress, ensure timely follow-ups, and reflect on feedback received. Ultimately, being organized contributes to a more effective and successful job search.

Practical Exercise with Examples:

Create a logbook. Dedicate a page for each job you have applied for so that you can keep notes of every step of the way. Keep notes on whether you landed an interview or not. Write down your thoughts on the job and what you felt might be a good match or where your weaknesses may have been. This will help you to see where you may need improvement. This logbook will also help you to review past contacts and see if you are able to reapply to any companies where you may have needed more training or experience or just didn't fit in at that time.

Example: Logbook Page 1

**Company**: ABC Company
**Position**: Systems Analyst

| Date | Applied/Interview/Follow-up | Notes |
|------|------------------------------|-------|
| 1/6/22 | Applied | They wanted someone with CISCO certification which I don't have but I have experience. |
| 1/21/22 | Interview-HR, 2pm CST, with Allison Carter | HR called me for a quick interview. Interview went well but it seems they want someone with more experience with networks. |
| 1/22/22 | | Sent thank you letter to Allison Carter for taking the time to reach out to me. |
| 2/22/22 | | Never heard back |

Example: Logbook Page 2/3

&lt;Copy of resume – dated 2/26/22&gt;

Example: Logbook Page 4

**Company**: XYZ Company
**Position**: Systems Analyst

| Date | Applied/Interview/Follow-up | Notes |
|------|------------------------------|-------|
| 3/2/22 | Applied | I meet most of the qualifications they are looking for. |
| 3/6/22 | | Received an email to setup interview with HR. On 3/8 at 1pm. |
| 3/8/22 | Interview-HR, 1pm CST, with Jake Daniels | The interview went well; He said the next step was to interview with the hiring Manager. |
| 3/9/22 | | Sent Jake Daniels thank you letter thanking him for reaching out to me and it was a pleasure speaking with him. |
| 3/11/22 | Interview set up with Bob Rosa on 3/16 at 2:30pm. | Next interview setup with hiring manager. |
| 3/16/22 | Interview with Bob Rosa, 2:30pm CST | The interview went well; asked a lot about server management, if I'd done any work coordinating with dev teams; said there would be a lot of SQL work as well. I thought it went pretty well. ☺ |
| 3/16/22 | | Sent a thank you letter to Bob Rosa for taking his time to interview me and giving me opportunity to present myself. |
| 3/22/22 | Offer letter received | Yay! I start next week! Take copy of diploma and SS card. |
| 9/15/22 | | Sent me to 3-day CISCO Networks training class. |

Even after you have gotten a job, keep track of events and other changes in your work history in the logbook. Add notes on any training you have received or promotions and title changes. This book will become a good tool to refer to when looking back on your career or if you need to search for a new job.

## 3.3 Conclusion

Remember to use these online platforms and tools strategically. Focus on those most relevant to your industry and job search goals. Regularly update your profiles, stay engaged with relevant communities, and maintain a professional online presence to maximize your chances of securing the right job opportunities.

Remember, **a job search can take time, so remain persistent, proactive, and open to opportunities**. Continuously refine your strategy based on your experiences and adjust your approach as needed. Stay positive, maintain a professional demeanor, and leverage your network to enhance your job search efforts.

# Chapter 4: Leveraging the Power of Networking for Career Success

Networking is a fundamental component of career success, offering opportunities to connect with professionals, gain valuable insights, and uncover hidden job opportunities. In this chapter, we will explore the art of networking and provide you with actionable strategies to build a robust professional network. Whether you are a job seeker, a recent graduate, or an aspiring professional, mastering the art of networking will unlock doors to exciting career possibilities.

## 4.1 Understanding the Importance of Networking in Job Search

Networking is more than just exchanging business cards or adding connections on social media. It is about building meaningful relationships that can propel your career forward.

### 4.1.1 The Power of Connections

Here are some very good reasons for building a network within your profession.

1. **Opportunities**:

    A strong professional network opens doors to various opportunities, such as job leads, referrals, collaborations, partnerships, and mentorship. By connecting with individuals in your field, you increase your chances of discovering new career prospects and accessing hidden opportunities that may not be publicly advertised.

2. **Knowledge and Insights**:

    Networking provides an avenue to exchange knowledge, insights, and best practices with professionals who have expertise in your industry. Engaging with others allows you to stay updated on industry trends, advancements, and emerging technologies. It can also provide valuable advice and guidance from experienced individuals who have faced similar challenges and overcome them.

3. **Personal and Professional Growth**:

    Building a network fosters personal and professional growth by exposing you to diverse perspectives, ideas, and experiences. Interacting with professionals at different stages of their careers can inspire and motivate you to set higher goals and strive for excellence. Moreover, networking can provide opportunities for skill development, learning from others, and gaining valuable feedback on your own abilities and performance.

4. **Support and Collaboration:**

    A strong professional network provides a support system of like-minded individuals who understand the challenges and intricacies of your industry. When facing obstacles or seeking guidance, you can rely on your network for support, advice, and encouragement. Additionally, networking facilitates collaboration and the exchange of resources, enabling you to tackle projects, initiatives, or problems collectively, leading to enhanced outcomes.

## 5. Reputation and Visibility:

Building a network helps establish your professional reputation and increases your visibility within your industry. When you consistently engage with others, contribute to discussions, and provide value, you build a positive reputation as a knowledgeable and reliable professional. This can lead to recognition, referrals, and increased credibility among peers, employers, and potential clients or customers.

## 6. Long-Term Relationships:

Networking is about building meaningful relationships that extend beyond immediate benefits. By nurturing relationships with professionals in your field, you establish a strong foundation for long-term connections. These relationships can evolve into mentorships, partnerships, or collaborations that support your ongoing professional development and career progression.

Building a network within your profession is essential for accessing opportunities, gaining valuable insights, fostering personal and professional growth, receiving support, enhancing visibility, and establishing long-term relationships. **It is a strategic investment that can significantly propel your career forward and open doors to new possibilities**. Don't miss out on opportunities by skipping this step in your career growth or in life.

> Join online industry-specific forums, communities, and discussion boards specific to your industry or profession. These platforms, such as industry-specific subreddits, Quora, or professional forums, allow you to connect with experts, ask questions, and gain insights into the latest trends. Actively participating in discussions can help you expand your knowledge and network.

### 4.1.2 Overcoming Networking Challenges

Networking can be intimidating, especially for introverts or individuals new to the professional world. But each time you do it, it gets a little easier and before you know it, you can become a pro at making the connections you need to get ahead.

Keep in mind that we need to respect everyone's time and privacy when making connections. We should also respect others and speak with them in controlled and respectable tones.

When it comes to networking, several roadblocks can hinder the process and impact its effectiveness. Here are some common roadblocks to networking:

## 1. Lack of Confidence:

A lack of self-confidence can make it challenging to approach new people, strike up conversations, or effectively communicate your values. It may prevent you from taking the initiative to expand your network.

Sometimes your speech may cause you to feel insecure. Look for sites, family or friends who can help you improve your speech.

Example: https://www.linkedin.com/company/speeko/

## 2. Fear of Rejection:

The fear of being rejected or dismissed can discourage individuals from reaching out to others or attending networking events. This fear can hinder their ability to form new connections and seize potential opportunities.

## 3. Limited Time and Busy Schedules:

Busy work schedules and personal commitments can make it difficult to allocate dedicated time for networking activities. Limited availability can impede the ability to attend events, engage in follow-up conversations, or nurture relationships.

## 4. Unclear Goals and Expectations:

Networking without a clear purpose or goals can result in aimless interactions and limited outcomes. It is crucial to have a clear understanding of what you hope to achieve through networking and set realistic expectations.

## 5. Lack of Authenticity:

Trying to network by being overly transactional or insincere can create a barrier in building genuine connections. Authenticity is key in fostering trust and establishing long-term relationships with professionals in your network.

## 6. Networking in Comfort Zones:

Sticking only to familiar groups or known contacts can limit exposure to new opportunities and diverse perspectives. Stepping out of comfort zones and actively engaging with individuals outside of established networks is essential for growth.

## 7. Difficulty in Following Up:

Failure to follow up after initial interactions can hinder the progress of networking relationships. It is crucial to maintain communication, express gratitude, and nurture connections through ongoing conversations and meaningful engagement.

## 8. Lack of Preparation:

Insufficient preparation for networking events or conversations can lead to missed opportunities. Having a clear understanding of your own goals, interests, and value proposition can help you make a lasting impression and maximize networking potential.

Overcoming these roadblocks requires self-awareness, persistence, and a proactive approach. Building networking skills and gradually expanding comfort zones can help you navigate these challenges and unlock the benefits of effective networking.

To overcome networking roadblocks and approach networking with confidence and authenticity, consider implementing the following strategies:

1. **Set Clear Networking Goals:**
   Define your networking goals and objectives. Clarify what you hope to achieve through networking, whether it's expanding your professional contacts, seeking career advice, or exploring new opportunities. Having clear goals helps provide direction and purpose in your networking efforts.

2. **Practice Elevator Pitch:**
   Craft a concise and compelling elevator pitch that effectively communicates who you are, what you do, and what value you bring. Practice delivering it confidently, ensuring it highlights your unique skills, experiences, and interests. Remember to keep it short and easy to say.

3. **Build Self-Confidence:**
   Focus on building your self-confidence through self-assessment and personal development. Recognize your strengths, accomplishments, and unique qualities that make you valuable to others. Engage in activities that boost your self-esteem, such as public speaking or joining professional development programs.

4. **Start with Familiar Contacts:**
   Begin networking by reaching out to familiar contacts such as friends, colleagues, or classmates. This can help ease any initial discomfort and provide a supportive environment for practice and expanding your networking skills.

5. **Attend Networking Events:**
   Attend industry conferences, seminars, or meetups to connect with professionals in your field. Prepare ahead of time by researching the event and identifying key individuals or organizations you want to engage with. Approach conversations with genuine curiosity, actively listen, and ask insightful questions.

6. **Embrace Authenticity:**
   Be genuine and authentic when networking. Share your true passions, interests, and goals. Avoid trying to impress or portray yourself as someone you're not. Building authentic connections based on shared interests and values will foster stronger and more meaningful relationships.

7. **Follow Up and Stay Engaged:**
   After networking interactions, follow up with a personalized message or email to express gratitude and reinforce the connection. Stay engaged by periodically reaching out, sharing relevant resources, or inviting them to industry-related events. Nurture relationships by demonstrating genuine interest and providing support when appropriate.

**8. Seek Opportunities to Help Others:**

Networking is a two-way street. Look for opportunities to offer assistance, insights, or introductions to fellow professionals. Actively listen and identify how you can contribute to their success. Building a reputation as a helpful and supportive networker enhances your own credibility and fosters reciprocity.

Remember, overcoming networking roadblocks is an ongoing process. Continuously refine your networking skills, challenge yourself to step out of your comfort zone, and approach networking with a mindset of learning and building meaningful connections. With practice and persistence, you can develop confidence and authenticity in your networking endeavors.

## 4.2 Strategies to Build a Solid Foundation and Expanding Your Network

Building a solid foundation and expanding your network are essential strategies for professional growth and success. By establishing a strong base of connections and nurturing meaningful relationships, you open doors to new opportunities, insights, and support. In this topic, we will explore effective strategies and techniques to build a solid foundation and expand your network, empowering you to thrive in your career.

### 4.2.1 Defining Your Networking Goals

Before diving into networking activities, it is essential to define your goals. By identifying your objectives, whether it's expanding your industry knowledge, finding a mentor, or exploring new career paths, you can focus your networking efforts effectively.

To focus your networking efforts effectively, consider the following strategies:

**1. Define your objectives:**

Determine the specific goals you want to achieve through networking. Are you looking for career advancement, industry knowledge, mentorship, or business opportunities? Defining your objectives will help you direct your efforts towards the right connections and activities.

**2. Identify your target audience:**

Identify the individuals or groups within your profession who can help you achieve your networking objectives. This may include professionals in your field, industry leaders, potential mentors, colleagues, or alumni from your educational institution. Understanding your target audience will allow you to tailor your networking approach accordingly.

**3. Attend industry events and conferences:**

Actively participate in relevant industry events, conferences, seminars, and workshops. These gatherings provide opportunities to meet professionals, engage in conversations, and exchange ideas. Prioritize events that align with your goals and interests, as they are more likely to attract individuals who can contribute to your networking objectives.

## 4. Leverage online platforms:

Utilize professional networking platforms such as LinkedIn to connect with individuals in your field. Join industry-specific groups, participate in discussions, and share valuable content. Engage with other professionals through commenting, messaging, or offering assistance. Online platforms allow you to expand your network beyond geographical limitations and connect with professionals globally.

## 5. Seek introductions and referrals:

Leverage your existing connections to expand your network. Ask for introductions or referrals from trusted colleagues, mentors, or friends who may have connections in your target audience. Personal introductions often carry more weight and facilitate meaningful conversations.

## 6. Be proactive and engaged:

Actively engage in conversations and networking activities. Initiate discussions, ask thoughtful questions, and actively listen to others. Demonstrate your expertise and willingness to contribute to the professional community. Actively seeking out opportunities to connect and engage will yield more meaningful connections.

## 7. Offer value and assistance:

Networking is a two-way street. Look for ways to provide value to others in your network. Offer your expertise, share resources, or provide assistance when appropriate. By being generous and supportive, you build goodwill and strengthen your relationships.

## 8. Follow up and maintain relationships:

After making initial connections, follow up with individuals to express your appreciation for the interaction. Stay in touch by periodically reaching out, sharing relevant articles or resources, or inviting them for a coffee chat. Cultivate your relationships over time to ensure they remain strong and mutually beneficial.

Remember, networking is a continuous process, and it requires consistent effort and nurturing. Focus your networking efforts by aligning them with your objectives, targeting the right audience, and actively engaging with professionals in your field. By being strategic and intentional, you can maximize the benefits of networking and achieve your career goals.

Practical Exercise with Example:

Here's a practical example of how to start the networking process. You can use known associates or professionals on LinkedIn as a starting point and then move on to contacts in various companies.

Let's say you are interested in transitioning to a new role within the marketing field. Your objective is to connect with professionals who have experience in your desired role and industry. Here's a step-by-step approach to get started:

1. *Identify your target audience:*
    Research professionals who hold positions similar to your desired role or work in companies/industries that align with your interests. Use LinkedIn, industry directories, or professional association websites to find potential contacts.

2. *Utilize your existing network:*
    Check if you have any existing connections who can introduce you to individuals in your target audience. Reach out to colleagues, friends, or alumni who might have relevant connections and ask for introductions.

3. *Craft a personalized introduction message:*
    Once you have identified a potential contact, compose a concise and personalized message to introduce yourself. Mention how you found them and express your interest in their work or expertise. Highlight any common interests or connections to establish a rapport.

4. *Request a conversation or meeting:*
    Politely ask for a brief conversation, either in person, over the phone, or through a video call, to discuss their experiences and gain insights. Respect their time by suggesting a specific duration for the conversation (e.g., 15-20 minutes).

5. *Be flexible and accommodating:*
    If the person agrees to connect with you, be accommodating and flexible with scheduling the conversation. Offer multiple time options and let them choose what works best for them.

6. *Prepare for the conversation:*
    Prior to the conversation, research the person's background, company, and any recent projects they have worked on. Prepare a list of questions related to their career journey, industry trends, or advice for someone aspiring to enter the field.

7. *Engage in the conversation:*
    During the conversation, be attentive, actively listen, and ask thoughtful questions. Show genuine interest in their experiences and insights. Be prepared to share a bit about yourself and your career aspirations but keep the focus primarily on learning from their expertise.

8. *Follow up and express gratitude:*
    After the conversation, promptly send a personalized thank-you email expressing your gratitude for their time and insights. Mention any key takeaways from the conversation and express your willingness to stay connected.

9. *Maintain the relationship:*
    Keep the connection alive by periodically staying in touch. Share relevant articles, industry updates, or resources that might be of interest to them. Attend industry events or webinars where you might cross paths with them. Look for opportunities to support and engage with them professionally.

By following these steps, you can start the networking process and start building relationships with professionals in your desired field. Remember, networking is a long-term endeavor, so approach it with sincerity, patience, and a willingness to give back to the professional community.

### 4.2.3 Enhancing Your Personal Brand

**Your personal brand is a reflection of your professional identity and plays a crucial role in networking**. It is important that you develop a strong personal brand by identifying your unique strengths, values, and expertise and then showcase it through various channels, including social media platforms and professional networking websites.

## 4.3 Expanding Your Network

In the digital age, online platforms offer vast networking opportunities. Platforms such as LinkedIn are a great place to start to build your network and expand on it. You must stay connected, engage with relevant communities, and have relevant information on your own profile. Make sure to always have updated information on your profile.

There are also live events that one can attend to increase access to other professionals in your area or trade. These events are often advertised in industry specific magazines and social media sites. Don't miss these great opportunities to find other like-minded people and professionals.

There are also virtual events that one can attend as well. Again, you can find these advertised in trade journals, publications, newspapers, and social media.

## 4.4 Nurturing Relationships and Leveraging Connections

Cultivating relationships is crucial both in your professional journey and personal life. Whether you are pursuing your career goals or engaging in personal endeavors, establishing connections with individuals who share similar interests, such as professionals, mentors, students, and more, holds immense value. These connections provide avenues for expanding your horizons, gaining diverse perspectives, and enhancing your overall life experiences. Moreover, once these relationships are established, it is important to actively nurture and cultivate them to unlock their full potential.

### 4.4.1 Building Meaningful Relationships

Networking is not merely about collecting business cards or adding connections on social media. It is about building meaningful, mutually beneficial relationships with professionals in your industry or field. By cultivating genuine connections, you create a network that can provide support, opportunities, and valuable insights throughout your career.

Networking goes beyond mere transactional interactions and revolves around establishing genuine connections that are meaningful and mutually advantageous. By focusing on relationship-building, you can create a strong and supportive network.

Here are some strategies to cultivate these genuine connections.

1. **Active Listening:**
   Active listening is a fundamental aspect of building meaningful relationships. When engaging with others, make a conscious effort to truly listen and understand what they are saying. Show genuine interest by asking thoughtful questions and seeking to comprehend their perspectives. This demonstrates respect and fosters a deeper connection with the other person.

2. **Offering Support:**
   Networking involves more than just seeking personal gain; it's about offering support and assistance to others in your network. Look for opportunities to provide value and help others succeed. This can be sharing relevant resources, offering advice or expertise, or making introductions to individuals who can contribute to their goals. By being a helpful and reliable resource, you build trust and strengthen the relationships within your network.

3. **Providing Value:**
   Look for ways to provide value to your network. Share industry insights, articles, or helpful information that aligns with their interests. Offer your expertise or skills to assist others in achieving their objectives. By consistently providing value, you establish yourself as a valuable connection and someone others can rely on. This fosters reciprocity within the network and strengthens the bonds between professionals.

4. **Building Relationships, Not Transactions:**
   Networking should not be approached as a series of transactional interactions solely focused on immediate gain. Instead, concentrate on building authentic relationships based on trust, respect, and shared interests. Take the time to get to know individuals on a personal level, beyond their professional achievements. Show empathy, celebrate their successes, and provide support during challenging times. By investing in genuine relationships, you create a supportive network that is there for you and willing to collaborate.

5. **Nurturing Relationships Over Time:**
   Building relationships requires ongoing effort and nurturing. It's essential to stay connected and engaged with your network. Regularly reach out to individuals, whether it's through occasional catch-up meetings, virtual coffee chats, or attending industry events together. Show genuine interest in their lives and careers. By maintaining the connection, you ensure that your network remains strong and supportive.

**By focusing on relationship-building rather than transactional interactions, you cultivate a network that is genuinely invested in your success.** Active listening, offering support, providing value, and nurturing relationships over time are key strategies for cultivating meaningful connections. Networking becomes a mutually beneficial endeavor where professionals support and uplift one another, creating a strong and supportive network that can propel collective growth and success.

## 4.4.2 The Power of Mentorship

Mentorship plays a vital role in professional growth, providing numerous benefits and opportunities for career advancement. Here's an expansion on the topic, discussing the benefits of having a mentor, guidance on finding a suitable mentor, establishing a productive mentor-mentee relationship, and leveraging your mentor's guidance:

*Benefits of Having a Mentor*

1. **Guidance and Wisdom:**

   A mentor offers valuable guidance based on their experiences and expertise. They can provide insights into navigating challenges, making important decisions, and overcoming obstacles in your professional journey.

2. **Knowledge and Skill Development:**

   Mentors can share their knowledge, industry-specific skills, and best practices. They provide practical advice, offer learning opportunities, and help you develop the necessary competencies to excel in your field.

3. **Networking and Connections:**

   Mentors often have extensive networks and can introduce you to key individuals within your industry. They can provide valuable connections, open doors to new opportunities, and expand your professional network.

4. **Increased Confidence and Self-Awareness:**

   Mentors offer support, encouragement, and feedback, helping you build confidence in your abilities. They can also provide constructive criticism and help you identify areas for growth, promoting self-awareness and personal development.

*Finding a Suitable Mentor*

1. **Look within your Network:**

   Start by identifying professionals within your existing network who possess the skills, knowledge, or expertise you seek. They can be colleagues, supervisors, or industry contacts. Reach out to them and express your interest in establishing a mentoring relationship.

2. **Industry Associations and Networks:**

   Join industry associations or professional networks that offer mentoring programs. These programs match mentees with experienced professionals who are willing to share their knowledge and support others' growth.

3. **Alumni Networks:**

   Explore alumni networks of your educational institutions. Alumni who are further along in their careers and have achieved success in your desired field can be valuable mentors.

*Establishing a Productive Mentor-Mentee Relationship*

### 1. Clear Expectations:
Establish clear expectations and goals for the mentoring relationship. Discuss what you hope to achieve, the frequency and format of meetings, and the preferred communication channels. Ensure both parties have a shared understanding of the commitment involved.

### 2. Open Communication:
Maintain open and honest communication with your mentor. Share your aspirations, challenges, and areas where you seek guidance. Be receptive to feedback and actively seek advice and input from your mentor.

### 3. Respect and Appreciation:
Show respect for your mentor's time, expertise, and guidance. Express gratitude for their support, acknowledging the value they bring to your professional development.

*Leveraging Your Mentor's Guidance*

### 1. Act on Feedback:
Actively incorporate feedback and advice provided by your mentor into your professional practices. Implement their suggestions, apply their insights, and monitor your progress.

### 2. Seek Learning Opportunities:
Request recommendations for relevant books, courses, or workshops to enhance your skills. Leverage your mentor's knowledge to identify valuable learning resources.

### 3. Expand Your Network:
Take advantage of your mentor's network by attending industry events together or seeking introductions to key professionals. Build relationships within your mentor's circle to further broaden your connections.

Remember, mentorship is a mutually beneficial relationship. While mentors provide guidance and support, it's important to demonstrate your commitment, actively engage, and utilize the advice and insights they offer. By leveraging mentorship, you can accelerate your professional growth, gain valuable insights, and enhance your career trajectory.

## 4.5 Conclusion:
Keep in mind that networking extends beyond personal gains; it involves nurturing genuine connections, offering assistance, and delivering value to others. Embrace networking as an ongoing journey, approaching it with sincerity, inquisitiveness, and a true intention to build authentic relationships.

# Chapter 5: Leveraging Online Platforms and Tools

In today's market, leveraging online platforms and tools is essential for maximizing the effectiveness of your job search efforts. **A strong professional online presence using platforms like LinkedIn will showcase you as a prospective candidate to a future employer.** Optimize your profile with relevant keywords, showcase your skills and experiences, and engage with industry content. Share thought leadership articles, insights, and relevant news to position yourself as a knowledgeable professional in your field.

Make use of online job boards to find prospective employers. Interact with others on social media that is relevant to your industry. Use training platforms to learn new things in your field or simply revise your knowledge on something you know but might need additional reinforcement on. The tools are there to support you on your journey.

## 5.1 Optimizing Your LinkedIn Profile

Optimizing your LinkedIn profile is crucial for creating a strong professional online presence. Many prospective employers can often use this tool to look up or search for future employees.

Here are some ways you can optimize your LinkedIn profile.

1. **Use a professional profile photo:**
   Choose a high-quality, recent photo that presents you in a professional manner. A friendly and approachable expression is recommended.

2. **Write a compelling headline:**
   Your headline appears under your name and should provide a concise and attention-grabbing summary of your professional identity, expertise, or current role. Make it keyword-rich and specific to your industry.

3. **Craft a compelling summary:**
   Use the summary section to highlight your unique value proposition and key skills. Write a concise and engaging summary that showcases your achievements, experiences, and career aspirations. Use relevant keywords to increase visibility in searches.

4. **Customize your URL:**
   Edit your LinkedIn profile URL to include your name or a variation of it. This helps create a clean and professional URL that is easy to share.

5. **Optimize your job descriptions:**
   For each position you list, provide detailed descriptions of your roles, responsibilities, and accomplishments. Use action verbs, quantify achievements when possible, and highlight specific skills and outcomes.

## 6. Showcase your skills and endorsements:

List your key skills in the designated section and encourage colleagues and connections to endorse you for those skills. Be sure to include skills that are relevant to your industry and expertise.

## 7. Add multimedia content:

Enhance your profile by including relevant multimedia content such as videos, presentations, or projects. This can provide a visual representation of your work and make your profile more engaging.

## 8. Include relevant keywords:

Incorporate industry-specific keywords throughout your profile to improve searchability. This includes your headline, summary, job descriptions, and skills section.

## 9. Request recommendations:

Reach out to former colleagues, supervisors, or clients and ask them to provide recommendations that highlight your strengths and expertise. Authentic recommendations add credibility to your profile.

## 10. Join relevant groups and engage with content:

Participate in industry-related LinkedIn groups to expand your network and demonstrate your knowledge and expertise. Engage with content by liking, commenting, and sharing relevant posts.

## 11. Regularly update your profile:

Keep your LinkedIn profile up to date by adding new skills, experiences, certifications, or projects. Stay active on the platform by sharing industry news, insights, or articles to showcase your engagement and expertise.

## 12. Make your profile public:

Ensure that your profile is visible to the public so that it can be discovered by recruiters, potential clients, or collaborators. Adjust your privacy settings accordingly.

Remember, your LinkedIn profile is an online representation of your professional identity. Regularly review and update your profile to reflect your current skills, experiences, and career goals.

As of this writing, LinkedIn has an AI tool that can help you optimize your profile and perform other career related tasks such as writing cover letters or filing in applications automatically. Give it a try.

https://chrome.google.com/webstore/detail/careerflow-ai-linkedin-op/iadokddofjgcgjpjlfhngclhpmaelnli

Similar to ChatGPT, Grammarly (https://www.grammarly.com/) can help you to write better introductions and summaries or help you to write a cover letter or an elevator pitch that sounds more professional.

Practical Exercise:

Take this moment to examine your LinkedIn profile. Evaluate how others in your profession have showcased themselves and take some pointers from them to update your profile. Also look to see what others are posting and try to repost with your own insights into the topic being discussed. By engaging with other posts, you open yourself to new connections and also show your efforts at engaging with the community you are involved with.

## 5.2 Harnessing the Power of Professional Social Media

Harnessing the power of professional social media platforms, such as LinkedIn, can provide numerous benefits for your career and professional development.

Here are some ways you can leverage the power of professional social media.

1. **Build a strong professional network:**
   Connect with colleagues, industry professionals, mentors, and thought leaders in your field. Expand your network by actively seeking out relevant connections and engaging with their content.

   > Besides LinkedIn, explore other professional networking platforms that cater to specific industries or professional communities. Examples include Behance for creatives, GitHub for developers, and Dribble for designers. Join relevant groups, engage in discussions, and showcase your work to connect with industry professionals and potential employers.

2. **Showcase your expertise:**
   Share valuable insights, industry knowledge, and thought leadership content through posts, articles, or comments. Demonstrate your expertise and establish yourself as a credible professional in your field.

3. **Engage in discussions and conversations:**
   Participate in industry-related discussions and engage with other professionals' content. Offer meaningful contributions, ask questions, and provide valuable insights to establish yourself as an active and knowledgeable member of the community.

   > Leverage social media platforms beyond LinkedIn to boost your job search. Follow and engage with companies you are interested in on platforms like Twitter or Instagram. Share

### 4. Stay informed about industry trends and news:

Follow industry influencers, companies, and organizations to stay up to date with the latest trends, news, and developments in your field. Share relevant articles or news updates with your network to showcase your industry knowledge.

### 5. Seek career opportunities:

Utilize professional social media platforms to explore job opportunities, connect with recruiters, and stay updated on the latest job postings in your industry. Create a well-crafted profile that highlights your skills and experiences to attract potential employers.

### 6. Join relevant groups and communities:

Participate in industry-specific groups and communities to connect with like-minded professionals, share insights, and learn from others in your field. Actively engage in discussions and provide value to establish your presence and expand your network.

### 7. Seek and provide mentorship:

Use professional social media platforms to find mentors who can guide and support you in your career. Alternatively, offer mentorship to others based on your own experiences and expertise.

### 8. Showcase your work and achievements:

Share your professional accomplishments, projects, and success stories on your profile. Highlight your skills, certifications, and awards to demonstrate your capabilities and build credibility.

Make use of online portfolio platforms. If your work is visual or project-based, consider creating an online portfolio using platforms like Behance, Dribble, or Adobe Portfolio. Showcase your projects, skills, and expertise through a visually appealing and easily accessible portfolio. Include a link to your portfolio in your job applications to provide employers with a comprehensive view of your work. If you are a web developer, purchase a low budget site on GoDaddy or another host and create a site to showcase your eye for UI/UX.

### 9. Collaborate and seek partnerships:

Use social media platforms to identify potential collaborators, partners, or clients. Engage with professionals and companies whose values align with yours and explore collaboration opportunities.

10. **Attend virtual events and webinars:**
    Many professional social media platforms host virtual events, webinars, or workshops. Participate in these events to expand your knowledge, network with industry experts, and stay connected with the latest industry trends.

11. **Request and provide recommendations:**
    Request recommendations from colleagues, clients, or supervisors to strengthen your professional credibility. Offer recommendations to others whom you have worked with closely to build a strong professional network.

12. **Maintain professionalism and brand consistency:**
    Ensure that your online presence aligns with your professional image. Be mindful of the content you share, engage in respectful and constructive conversations, and maintain a consistent and professional tone across all interactions.

Remember to use professional social media platforms strategically and invest time in nurturing your online presence. Regularly update your profiles, engage with your network, and provide value to establish yourself as a respected professional in your field.

Resources:
These are just a few that are listed but there are many other sites that offer portfolio building capabilities.

> https://www.behance.net/
> https://dribbble.com/shots
> https://portfolio.adobe.com/
> https://www.wix.com/mystunningwebsites/hiker-portfolio
> https://www.web.com/website-builder-landing

## 5.3 Utilizing Job Search Platforms and Online Resources

Though the following may seem redundant, it is worth emphasizing again the importance of job search platforms and online resources, which can be valuable tools to help you find relevant job opportunities and support your job search efforts.

Here are some ways you can effectively use these platforms and resources.

1. **Identify reputable job search platforms:**
    Research and identify reputable job search platforms that are widely used in your industry or location. Popular platforms include LinkedIn, Indeed, Glassdoor, and CareerBuilder. Sign up for accounts and create detailed profiles to enhance your visibility to potential employers.

## 2. Refine your search criteria:

Utilize the advanced search filters provided by job search platforms to narrow down your job search based on specific criteria such as location, industry, job title, experience level, and salary range. Refining your search will help you find more relevant job listings.

## 3. Set up job alerts:

Take advantage of the job alert features offered by job search platforms. Set up alerts based on your desired job criteria, and you will receive notifications when new job opportunities that match your preferences are posted. This saves you time by delivering relevant job openings directly to your inbox.

## 4. Customize your resume and cover letter:

Tailor your resume and cover letter to each specific job application. Highlight your relevant skills, experiences, and achievements that align with the job requirements. Use keywords from the job description to optimize your resume for applicant tracking systems (ATS) used by employers.

## 5. Leverage your network:

Utilize professional networking platforms such as LinkedIn to connect with industry professionals, recruiters, and hiring managers. Actively engage in conversations, join relevant groups, and leverage your network for referrals and job leads. Let your connections know that you are actively seeking new opportunities.

## 6. Research companies and employers:

Use online resources like company websites, industry-specific websites, and social media platforms to research companies you are interested in. Gain insights into their culture, values, recent news, and employee experiences. This information can help you tailor your application and prepare for interviews.

## 7. Utilize company career pages:

Many companies have dedicated career pages on their websites where they post job openings. Regularly visit these pages, sign up for email notifications if available, and directly apply to positions of interest. Often, companies prioritize applications received through their career pages.

## 8. Explore industry-specific job boards:

Depending on your industry, there may be niche job boards or industry-specific websites that cater to specialized job opportunities. Research and explore these platforms to find job openings tailored to your field.

## 9. Attend virtual career fairs and webinars:

Online career fairs and webinars have become increasingly popular. Participate in these virtual events to connect with employers, learn about job opportunities, and gain insights from industry professionals. Prepare your elevator pitch and have your resume ready to share.

10. **Utilize professional development resources:**

    Online resources such as e-learning platforms, webinars, and industry publications can help you enhance your skills, stay updated on industry trends, and differentiate yourself from other job seekers. Invest time in relevant professional development activities to make yourself more attractive to employers.

11. **Seek advice and support:**

    Engage with online communities, forums, and career coaching platforms where you can seek advice, guidance, and support from experts and fellow job seekers. Utilize these resources to enhance your job search strategy, improve your application materials, and gain valuable insights.

## 5.4 Conclusion

Remember to stay organized during your job search process. Keep track of the jobs you have applied to, follow up on applications, and maintain a professional online presence. Regularly update your profiles, review feedback, and adjust your approach as needed. Persistence and consistency are key to a successful job search.

# Chapter 6: Mastering the Art of Resume Writing

Your resume is your first impression—a powerful tool that can open doors to exciting career opportunities. In this chapter, we will delve into the art of resume writing, equipping you with the knowledge and strategies to create a standout resume that grabs the attention of employers. From crafting a compelling summary to showcasing your accomplishments and tailoring your resume to specific job applications, you can start impressing a prospective employer with just your resume.

## 6.1 Understanding the Purpose of a Resume

Before we dive into the nitty-gritty details of resume writing, let's first understand the purpose and significance of this essential document.

### 6.1.1 The Power of First Impressions

Your resume is often the first point of contact between you and potential employers. It serves as a snapshot of your qualifications, experiences, and skills. By creating a well-crafted resume, you have the opportunity to make a positive first impression and pique the interest of the hiring managers.

### 6.1.2 Showcasing Your Value Proposition

A carefully constructed resume enables you to effectively communicate your unique value proposition—the specific skills, experiences, and qualities that make you an ideal candidate for a particular role. By strategically highlighting your accomplishments and aligning them with the requirements of the job, you can demonstrate your potential impact on the organization.

## 6.2 Structuring Your Resume

Once you have found one or more possible jobs, you will need to review the details of each job and tailor your resume and cover letter to meet the requirements.

Make sure to tailor your resume and cover letter for each application. Highlight relevant skills, experiences, and achievements that match the requirements of the job you're applying for. Use keywords from the job description to optimize your application for applicant tracking systems (ATS) and increase your chances of being noticed. We will discuss this in a later section.

### 6.2.1 Choosing the Right Resume Format

There are several resume formats to choose from, including chronological, functional, and combination formats. You will need to explore each format's advantages and determine which one best suit your unique circumstances.

While working on your resume, something to keep in mind is that certain positions, especially those advertised on government job sites, often require information about the number of hours worked per week to assess your level of experience. It is crucial to carefully review each site you are applying to, in order to grasp their specific requirements.

If you need assistance in creating a professional resume, utilize online resume builders such as Novoresume, Canva, ChatGPT, or Resume.io. These tools provide pre-designed templates and guidance to help you create a visually appealing and well-structured resume.

*Chronological Resume Format*
The chronological resume structure arranges your professional journey in a logical, time-based order, ensuring a coherent and easily comprehensible presentation. This format is widely embraced due to its simplicity, particularly when applying for roles closely aligned with one's work history. It showcases the specific responsibilities held in each role, providing clear insights into the chronology of achievements, and underlining professional growth.

# Sarah Wells
swells@info.ca | 212-555-1212 | Richmond, TX 77469

| | |
|---|---|
| **PROFESSIONAL SUMMARY** | IT professional with over 10 years of progressive experience in a variety of roles and functionality. My journey encompasses application design, development, testing, release processes and maintenance for projects of variable sizes, budgets, and timelines. |
| **KEY SKILLS** | • C#, VB, .NET • Business Analysis • SQL, Database Management • MS Office • Network Management • SharePoint • Active Domain Management • AWS |
| **EDUCATION** | **Master of Science CS**, Hunter College, NYC, 2020 **Bachelor of Science CS**, Adelphi, 2023 |
| **CERTIFICATIONS** | **Scrum Master Certification**, 2022 |
| **WORK HISTORY** | **Sr Analyst** | ABC Company - Edison, NJ | 05/2020 to Current • Served as primary liaison between client and internal teams. • Collaborated with teams, such as QA, support, stakeholders, and engineering, to ensure that tools and products were developed and delivered on time and within budget. • Lead, mentored, and managed software development teams working on various product lines. • Planned, scheduled, released, and managed multiple software projects, ensuring they were delivered on time and within budget. • Defined, designed, documented, and implemented software development best practices, methodologies, and processes to ensure efficient and high-quality product delivery. • Identified and managed risks and issues related to software development. **Sr SQL Developer** | Reuters – Hauppauge, NY | 01/2017 to 05/2020 • Tracked and reported on software development progress, spending, and metrics. • Developed database for financial tracking application. **QA Tester** | CompuServ – Los Angeles, CA | 05/2013 to 05/2017 • Created test case scenarios for various applications and developed technical documents to accurately define test cases. • Performed API testing, website testing and application testing. |

*Example Chronological Resume Format*

Take this moment to work on your resume using the chronological format. Use notes you took throughout section 1 to help you organize the various sections of the resume. Writing a resume takes time so don't get discouraged if you get stuck. Go away for a bit and then come back to work on it again.

## Functional Resume Format

While many individuals opt for chronological resumes to underscore their career progression, there are scenarios where alternative formats might be more suitable. If you are a newcomer to the job market, have encountered career gaps, navigated through temporary positions, or are endeavoring to change your career path, the functional resume could be the more fitting choice. This style of resume emphasizes your competencies, prioritizing skill sets over a strict chronological presentation of experiences.

# Sarah Wells

**CONTACT**
Richmond, TX 77469
212-555-1212
swells@info.ca

**SKILLS**
-C#, VB, .NET
-SQL
-Network Mgmt

**EDUCATION**
BA CS, Adelphi, 2023

**CERTIFICATIONS**
Scrum Master
Certification, 2022

**PROFESSIONAL SUMMARY**
IT professional with over 8 years of experience in application design, development, testing, release processes and maintenance for projects of variable sizes, budgets, and timelines.

**PROFESSIONAL SKILLS**
People Management

- Lead, mentored, and managed software development teams working on various product lines.
- Collaborated with other teams, such as QA, support, and engineering, to ensure that tools and products were developed and delivered on time and within budget.

Project Management

- Planned, scheduled, released, and managed multiple software projects, ensuring they were delivered on time and within budget.
- Defined, designed, documented, and implemented software development best practices, methodologies, and processes to ensure efficient and high-quality product delivery.
- Identified and managed risks and issues related to software development.
- Tracked and reported on software development progress, spending, and metrics.

Development

- Responsible for several web applications, including product analysis, development, testing and client interaction for timely deliverables.

**WORK HISTORY**
**Sr Analyst**, 05/2020 to Current
ABC Company – Edison, NJ

**Sr SQL Developer**, 01/2013 to 05/2018
Reuters – Hauppauge, NY

*Example Functional Resume Format*

Practical Exercise:

Using the chronological resume as a base, rearrange it and rewrite your resume using the functional format.

**Combined Resume Format**

For those with extensive and evolving career trajectories, executives aiming to frontload their qualifications, or individuals re-entering the workforce following a break, the combination resume presents itself as a prudent option. This hybrid format adeptly accentuates your pertinent skills upfront, followed by a strategic arrangement of your most relevant work experiences. Such a presentation delivers a powerful and balanced snapshot of your capabilities and professional history.

# Sarah Wells
swells@info.ca | 212-555-1212 | Richmond, TX 77469

| | |
|---|---|
| **PROFESSIONAL SUMMARY** | IT professional with over 8 years of progressive experience in a variety of roles and functionality. My journey encompasses application design, development, testing, release processes and maintenance for projects of variable sizes, budgets, and timelines. |
| **SUMMARY OF QUALIFICATIONS** | • Developed and executed a comprehensive product strategy aligned with the company's overall direction.<br>• Served as primary liaison between client and internal teams.<br>• Collaborated with teams, such as QA, support, stakeholders, and engineering, to ensure that tools and products were developed and delivered on time and within budget. |
| **KEY SKILLS** | • C#, VB, .NET     • Business Analysis<br>• SQL, Database Management     • MS Office<br>• Network Management     • SharePoint<br>• Active Domain Management     • AWS |
| **WORK HISTORY** | **Sr Analyst** \| ABC Company - Edison, NJ \| 05/2020 to Current<br>• Lead, mentored, and managed software development teams working on various product lines.<br>• Planned, scheduled, released, and managed multiple software projects, ensuring they were delivered on time and within budget.<br>• Defined, designed, documented, and implemented software development best practices, methodologies, and processes to ensure efficient and high-quality product delivery.<br>• Identified and managed risks and issues related to software development.<br><br>**Sr SQL Developer** \| Reuters – Hauppauge, NY \| 01/2013 to 05/2018<br>• Tracked and reported on software development progress, spending, and metrics.<br>• Developed database for financial tracking application. |
| **EDUCATION** | **Bachelor of Arts CS**, Adelphi, 2023 |
| **CERTIFICATIONS** | **Scrum Master** Certification, 2022 |

*Example Combination Resume Format*

Remember, no matter which resume format you begin with, don't hesitate to experiment with it. Tailor it to suit your needs and create a format that resonates best with your unique professional journey.

Practical Exercise:
Using the chronological resume and the functional resume, review the strengths from both and rewrite your resume using the combined format.

For more information on the different types of resumes, you may want to do additional reading here,
https://www.livecareer.com/resume/formats/combination
https://www.myperfectresume.com/

Here are some additional resources available online that can help you work on your resume. There are many more available.

https://novoresume.com/
https://www.myperfectresume.com/
https://resume.io/resume-templates
https://career.io/resume-builder
https://www.resumebuilder.com/
https://www.adobe.com/express/create/resume
https://www.Resumaker.ai

Remember while you are working on your resume that to ensure your resume effectively aligns with the digital era, it's important to optimize it for online applications and to guarantee readability across various devices.

## 6.2.2 Crafting an Attention-Grabbing Summary Statement
The summary statement is the first section of your resume, serving as a compelling introduction that captures the reader's attention. **Use the summary section to draw attention to your main qualifications**. Keep it short but concise.

## 6.2.3 Highlighting Your Professional Experience
The professional experience section is where you can showcase your career trajectory, responsibilities, and achievements. Use this section to highlight all those points that the employer is looking for and customize it with your experiences. Make sure to emphasize your accomplishments using key actional words and quantify your results for a bigger impact. Make sure that your experiences align to the job requirements. This will reinsure you and the employer that you have the experience needed to do the job.

## 6.2.4 Showcasing Your Education and Certifications
Your educational background and relevant certifications play a vital role in your resume. For students this is where you can highlight relevant coursework, honors, and certifications that align with the target role you are applying for.

### 6.2.5 Mentioning Extracurricular Activities

Make sure to include any relevant extracurricular activities when applying for the position. For instance, if you hold a board member position in a school or company, certain employers may be interested in your experience in making important decisions for a governing body. Similarly, if you engage in non-profit work, such as fundraising or assisting people in need, it showcases your empathy and altruistic nature. If your resume allows for a free form section, this area can be an excellent platform to emphasize your non-job-related activities and contributions.

## 6.3 Tailoring Your Resume for Success

To maximize the impact of your resume, it is crucial to tailor it to the specific job you are applying for.

### 6.3.1 Analyzing Job Descriptions

Your first step is to find the job description that you are applying for.  Analyzing the job descriptions is a crucial step in the job search process. It allows you to understand the specific skills, qualifications, and experiences sought by hiring managers. Make sure to include your unique selling points (Leadership, Problem-solving, Communication, Adaptable, Cross-cultural Competence and Innovative) and highlight your transferable skills (communication, problem-solving, leadership, teamwork, adaptability, and critical thinking).

By thoroughly analyzing job descriptions and tailoring your application to align with the requirements, will increase your chances of capturing the attention of hiring managers.

Here are some ways you can improve and tune your resume to the job you are applying for.

1. **Read the job description thoroughly:**
   Begin by carefully reading the job description from start to finish. Pay attention to the language used, the required qualifications, and the responsibilities outlined. Gain a clear understanding of what the employer is seeking in an ideal candidate.

   In some cases, it might be necessary to investigate the role as it is commonly defined within your industry. This will provide you with valuable insights into additional skills you may require or already possess, which you can then emphasize.

2. **Identify key requirements:**
   Highlight or make a list of the key requirements mentioned in the job description. These can include specific technical skills, years of experience, educational qualifications, certifications, or desired personal attributes.

   Remember your unique selling points: Leadership, Problem-solving, Communication, Adaptable, Cross-cultural Competence and Innovative.

   Make sure to be concise and to the point on each item you enter.  Too many words can distract the reader and force them to move on to the next resume.

3. **Assess your qualifications:**

Evaluate your own qualifications and experiences in relation to the identified key requirements. Take note of the skills, experiences, and achievements that directly match or closely align with what the job description is seeking.

If you're considering a career change or returning to the job market after a hiatus, you might worry that your skills aren't up to date. However, this isn't necessarily the case. Utilize your transferable skills and emphasize their relevance to the skills employers are seeking. Many jobs share common elements, and what sets them apart is often subject matter expertise. You can assure the employer that you can align with the required skill set for the job and quickly acquire the specific subject matter knowledge needed.

4. **Customize your application:**

Tailor your resume, cover letter, and any other application materials to emphasize your relevant qualifications. Highlight the skills, experiences, and achievements that directly align with the identified key requirements from the job description. Provide specific examples and measurable results whenever possible.

Ensure that you incorporate the company's name and the job title in your cover letter. Utilize numerical data to quantify your achievements in previous roles, demonstrating how you made improvements. While keeping your resume concise, employ numbers and percentages to underscore your capacity for productivity and efficiency.

5. **Showcase your accomplishments:**

When discussing your previous work experiences, focus on highlighting accomplishments and outcomes that demonstrate your ability to meet the key requirements. Quantify your achievements and use action verbs to convey impact.

| | | |
|---|---|---|
| *Accomplished* | *Contributed* | *Enhanced* |
| *Generated* | *Improved* | *Increased* |
| *Renovated* | *Revamped* | *Streamlined* |
| *Produced* | *Earned* | *Influenced* |

6. **Address any gaps:**

If there are certain requirements in the job description that you don't meet, consider how you can address them. Highlight transferable skills or experiences that can compensate for any gaps. Express your willingness to learn and adapt to new challenges.

Career breaks should not be viewed negatively. Many employers are primarily interested in understanding how you utilized that time away from work to achieve various goals, whether they were personal or professional. They seek assurance that you were engaged and productive during that period.

## 7. Research the company culture:

Alongside the key requirements, also pay attention to any hints about the company culture or values embedded in the job description. Aligning your application with these aspects can further demonstrate your fit and enthusiasm for the organization.

## 8. Proofread and polish:

Before submitting your application, proofread it thoroughly to ensure there are no errors or inconsistencies. Polish your application materials to present yourself as a strong candidate who has taken the time to tailor their application to the specific job requirements.

By effectively analyzing the job description and identifying the key requirements and aligning your qualifications accordingly, you enhance your chances of standing out to hiring managers. By showcasing your relevant skills and experiences, you demonstrate your suitability for the role and increase your likelihood of being invited for an interview. It also shows that you are not just sending a generic resume to every job you are applying for.

### 6.3.2 Incorporating Keywords

Many companies utilize applicant tracking systems (ATS) to screen resumes. It is very important to make use of relevant keywords throughout your resume to ensure it passes through ATS filters. Use dictionaries and thesauruses to identify keywords and seamlessly integrate them into your document. Don't copy word for word what's on the job description but rephrase some of the main points to meet the job requirements.

> To increase the chances of your resume getting noticed, tailor it to match the keywords and requirements specified in the job description. Use online tools like Jobscan (jobscan.co) or SkillSyncer (skillsyncer.com) to analyze your resume against job descriptions and optimize it for ATS. Submit customized resumes to prospective employers to show you are paying attention to the details.

Resources:

Here are some resources. You can Google for more sites that can further help.

https://www.jobscan.co/lp/ats-wrapper-2
https://resumegenius.com/blog/resume-help/ats-resume
https://www.coursera.org/articles/resume-action-words

> Transferable skills are valuable assets that can be applied across different roles and industries. Make sure to incorporate these skills throughout the resume for bigger impact.

## 6.4 Perfecting the Details

Perfecting the details of resumes is a crucial aspect of creating a strong impression on potential employers. Paying attention to formatting, grammar, and content ensures that your resume effectively showcases your qualifications and experiences. In this topic, we will delve into the key elements of resume refinement, providing guidance on how to enhance your resume's impact and increase your chances of securing desired opportunities.

### 6.4.1 Formatting and Design

An effective resume goes beyond presenting your qualifications and experiences; it captivates the reader's attention and leaves a positive impact. It is visually appealing, easy to read, and typically spans around 1-2 pages. A well-designed resume conveys essential information in a straightforward yet visually pleasing format, allowing the reader to grasp important details without searching extensively. Crafting a compelling resume requires time, practice, and sometimes guidance from experienced writers.

Consider the following formatting techniques, font choices, layout considerations, and visual elements to enhance the aesthetics of your document.

1. **Formatting Techniques:**
   - Use consistent formatting throughout the resume, including font size, spacing, and margins.
   - Utilize headings, subheadings, and bullet points to create a clear and organized structure.
   - Incorporate white space strategically to improve readability and avoid clutter.
   - Employ bold or italics to emphasize key points, such as job titles or notable achievements.

2. **Font Choices:**
   - Select professional, easy-to-read fonts such as Arial, Calibri, or Times New Roman.
   - Use a larger font size for section headings (e.g., Contact Information, Work Experience) to create visual hierarchy.
   - Maintain consistency in font styles and sizes throughout the document for a polished look.

3. **Layout Considerations:**
   - Opt for a clean and uncluttered layout that allows for easy scanning of information.
   - Arrange sections in a logical order, starting with your contact information followed by a summary/objective, work experience, education, and relevant skills.
   - Align text and headings consistently to create a visually pleasing flow.
   - Consider a two-column format for certain sections, such as skills or qualifications, to maximize space and readability.

4. **Visual Elements:**
   - Incorporate icons or symbols to represent different sections or skills, adding visual interest and aiding in information categorization.
   - Use infographics or charts to visually represent quantifiable achievements or skills, making them more impactful and memorable.

- Include a professional headshot if it aligns with industry standards and enhances your personal brand.

5. **Words, Words, and Words:**
   - Use adjectives and verbs that show impact.
   - Use the descriptions for the job and tailor it to your experience.
   - Use proactive words that give positive vibes and not negative or doubtful vibes.

Example – Resume utilizing applicant tracking systems (ATS) techniques.

---

# Sherry Lewis

**/in/sherrylewis** | slewis@example-site.com

A highly motivated and results-driven marketing professional with a proven track record in digital marketing strategies and campaign management. Passionate about leveraging data-driven insights to drive brand awareness and customer engagement.

**Work Experience:**
**Marketing Specialist** | XYZ Company | 02/05/2020- present
- Implemented targeted digital marketing campaigns resulting in a 20% increase in website traffic and a 15% boost in lead generation.
- Coordinated social media content strategy, resulting in a 50% growth in followers and a 25% increase in engagement rate.

**Technical Writer** | Adobe | 05/13/2013 – 12/22/2019
- Provided the necessary updates, documentation, and provisions to apply for and maintain PCI-DSS compliance with Visa and Wells Fargo for safe and secure credit card processing.

**Education:**
**Bachelor of Business Administration in Marketing** | ABC University | 2023

**Skills:**
- Digital Marketing (SEO, SEM, PPC)
- Social Media Management
- Google Analytics
- Content Creation and Copywriting

**Professional Development:**
*Certifications:* Google Ads, HubSpot Inbound Marketing
*Workshops:* Advanced Social Media Strategies, Data-Driven Marketing

*References available upon request.*

---

In this example, the resume utilizes a clean layout with consistent formatting. Section headings are bolded, and bullet points are used to convey achievements and responsibilities. The skills section highlights the different skills, enhancing readability. Overall, the resume presents information in a visually appealing and well-structured manner, making it easy for the reader to navigate and comprehend.

Resources.

https://www.jobscan.co/blog/top-resume-keywords-boost-resume/
https://www.indeed.com/career-advice/resumes-cover-letters/resume-keywords-and-phrases

### 6.4.2 Proofreading and Editing

Attention to detail is crucial when it comes to your resume.

It is essential that you proofread your document and even get assistance from friends and family or colleagues to make sure it is up to par. Ensure that your resume is error-free and polished. From grammar and spelling to consistency and clarity, you must check all aspects of your document to make a strong first impression.

Here's an elaboration on the importance of attention to detail in your resume, along with an example:

**Attention to detail is paramount when it comes to your resume.** It demonstrates your professionalism, meticulousness, and commitment to presenting your qualifications accurately. To ensure your resume is error-free and polished, it's essential to apply essential proofreading and editing techniques. By reviewing your document thoroughly, you can address grammar and spelling errors, ensure consistency, and enhance clarity. Here's an example that highlights the importance of attention to detail:

Example:

---

[Your Name]
[Contact Information]

Profesional Summary:
A results-oriented marketing professional with expertise in developing and executing successful digital marketing campaigns. Proven track record of driving brand awareness, increasing online engagement, and delivering measurable results.

Work Experience:
Digital Marketing Specialist | XYZ Company | Dates
- Developed, implemented comprehensive digital marketing strategies, resulting in a 25% increase in website traffic and a 15% boost in lead generation.
- Managed social media channels, curating engaging content that drove a 40% growth in followers and 20% increase in customer engagement.

Education:
Bachelor of Business Administration in Marketing | ABC University | Year

---

Skills:
- Digital Marketing (SEO, SEM, PPC)
- Social Media Management
- Google Analytics
- Content Creation and Copywriting

At first glance, the example looks okay. But with further perusal we can find a few syntax errors and we can find a better way to present the candidate.  Following is a more polished version:

[Your Name]
[Contact Information]

**Professional** Summary:
A results-oriented marketing professional with expertise in developing and executing successful digital marketing campaigns. **I have** a proven track record of driving brand awareness, increasing online engagement, and delivering measurable results.

Work Experience:
Digital Marketing Specialist | XYZ Company | Dates
- **Designed,** Developed, **and I**mplemented comprehensive digital marketing strategies, resulting in a 25% increase in website traffic and a 15% boost in lead generation.
- Managed social media channels, curating engaging content that drove a 40% growth in followers and **a** 20% increase in customer engagement.

Education:
Bachelor of Business Administration in Marketing | ABC University | Year

Skills:
- Digital Marketing (SEO, SEM, PPC)
- Social Media Management
- Google Analytics
- Content Creation and Copywriting

In this example, attention to detail is crucial to ensure accuracy and professionalism. The corrected and polished version of the resume eliminates any grammatical or spelling errors, ensuring clear communication of your qualifications. Consistency is maintained in the formatting and structure of the document. The revised version presents a more polished and error-free resume, making a strong impression on the reader.

By paying careful attention to detail, you can ensure your resume is error-free, consistent, and clear. Reviewing your document thoroughly for grammar, spelling, consistency, and clarity allows you to present yourself professionally and make a positive impact on potential employers.

### 6.4.3 Application Tracking System- ATS

Many companies have resorted to using Applicant Tracking Systems (ATS) to help them filter and screen job applicants when trying to fill a position in the company. These systems are often used to parse out resumes, pick out key words for specific jobs from the resumes, create candidate profiles that it then uses to profile incoming resumes and will often create a list of the most viable candidates who have submitted their resumes.  It would be wise to create an ATS friendly resume so that your resume can be ultimately picked up for human perusal.

To ensure your resume gets through ATS and into the hands of a human recruiter, keep the following important factors in mind.

1. **Use Standard Formatting**: Stick to simple, standard formatting. Avoid using fancy fonts, graphics, or complex tables. Use a clean, easily readable font (e.g., Arial, Calibri, Garamond, Helvetica, Georgia, et al) and keep the layout straightforward.

2. **Use Appropriate Headings**: Use clear and standard headings for sections like "Work Experience," "Education," "Skills," and "Contact Information." Avoid creative or unusual section titles that might confuse the ATS.

3. **Include Relevant Keywords**: Carefully read the job description and incorporate relevant keywords and phrases from it into your resume. These keywords should be naturally integrated into your skills, work experience, and qualifications.

4. **No Special Characters**: Avoid using special characters, symbols, or unusual formatting, as these can confuse ATS software. Stick to standard characters and bullet points.

5. **Save in a Common File Format**: Save your resume in a common file format like .docx or .pdf. Some ATS systems can have trouble parsing other file types.

6. **Use a Logical Structure**: Organize your resume logically with clear headings and consistent formatting. Start with your contact information, followed by a summary or objective statement (if desired), and then move on to sections like work experience, education, skills, and certifications. Make sure to keep it as chronologically correct as possible.

7. **Focus on Text:** Avoid embedding important information within images, logos, or other non-text elements. ATS can't read text within images.

8. **Spell Out Acronyms:** While you may be familiar with industry-specific acronyms, it's best to spell them out in your resume at least once, followed by the acronym in parentheses (e.g., Customer Relationship Management (CRM), Enterprise Resource Planning (ERP)).

9. **Check for Consistency**: Ensure consistent use of tense, formatting, and abbreviations throughout your resume. ATS systems can be sensitive to inconsistencies.

10. **Customize for Each Job**: Tailor your resume for each specific job application. This includes adjusting your list of skills, qualifications, and relevant experience to align with the job description.

11. **Include Relevant Details**: Include relevant details such as job titles, dates of employment, company names, and education institutions. ATS systems use this information to categorize and rank applicants.

12. **Avoid Uncommon Fonts:** Stick to widely recognized and available fonts, as ATS may have trouble reading less common ones.

13. **Test Your Resume**: Before submitting your resume, use an ATS-friendly resume scanner or checker available online. These tools can help you identify potential issues and ensure your resume is optimized for ATS.

Some testers are listed here.
> https://www.jobscan.co/resume-scanner
> https://resumeworded.com/resume-scanner
> https://cultivatedculture.com/resume-scanner/

14. **Review for Readability**: After optimizing for ATS, review your resume to ensure it still reads well for humans. It should make sense and provide a clear picture of your qualifications.

By keeping these tips in mind, you can increase the chances of your resume successfully passing through ATS systems and reaching the hands of recruiters for further consideration. Remember that while ATS optimization is important, your resume should also effectively showcase your qualifications to human readers.

For further reading, refer to this link.

https://www.jobscan.co/blog/8-things-you-need-to-know-about-applicant-tracking-systems/

### 6.4.4 Crafting a Compelling Cover Letter
While not always mandatory, a well-crafted cover letter can significantly enhance your application by providing additional insights into your qualifications and motivations. It serves as a personalized introduction, allowing you to showcase your skills, experiences, and enthusiasm for the position.

Here are some reasons why a cover letter is so valuable.

1. **Personalization:**
> A cover letter enables you to tailor your application to the specific job and company. It gives you an opportunity to address the hiring manager directly, highlighting why you are interested in the role and how your qualifications align with their needs. Personalization demonstrates your genuine interest and dedication, setting you apart from other applicants.

## 2. Expanded Qualifications:

Your resume may provide a concise overview of your qualifications, but a cover letter allows you to expand on specific experiences, achievements, or skills that are relevant to the position. It provides context and elaboration, giving the hiring manager a deeper understanding of your capabilities and how they align with the job requirements.

## 3. Showcasing Your Motivations:

A cover letter provides a platform to express your motivations for applying to the role and the company. You can share why you are passionate about the industry, how the company's mission resonates with you, or how the position aligns with your long-term career goals. Sharing your motivations adds depth and authenticity to your application.

## 4. Addressing Potential Concerns:

If there are any aspects of your application that may raise questions or require clarification, a cover letter gives you an opportunity to address them proactively. Whether it's a career transition, a gap in employment, or a change in industries, you can provide context and reassure the hiring manager about your qualifications and suitability for the role.

## 5. Demonstrating Communication Skills:

A well-written cover letter showcases your communication skills and attention to detail. It allows you to demonstrate your ability to articulate your thoughts, organize information effectively, and present a persuasive argument for your candidacy. Strong communication skills are highly valued in many professions and can make a positive impression on employers.

When crafting a cover letter, ensure it is concise, well-structured, and tailored to the specific job and company. Address the hiring manager by name, if possible, and clearly state the position you are applying for. Highlight your relevant qualifications, experiences, and achievements, making connections between your skills and the job requirements. Finally, express your enthusiasm for the opportunity and thank the reader for their consideration.

It is also important to craft several versions of cover letters tailored to different levels of experience or positions within your industry. This proactive approach enables you to be ready to submit customized cover letters for specific job applications. For instance, if a job calls for a more junior level of experience and you're open to that role, it's more fitting to submit a cover letter tailored to a junior-level position rather than one highlighting extensive experience beyond the job's requirements. Likewise, a cover letter for a highly technical role like a programmer will significantly differ from one designed for a project manager position.

**It's important to know what audience you are applying to when writing your cover letter.**

While a cover letter may not always be required, taking the time to craft a well-tailored one can significantly enhance your application, demonstrate your qualifications and motivations, and increase your chances of standing out as a strong candidate.

Practical Exercise:
Write a few variances of cover letters for yourself for a few different positions and levels.

Practical Exercise:
Once you have gathered the different artifacts for your career, you should consider digitizing them to ensure their accessibility when applying for jobs online. It's not only crucial to have your resumes and cover letters readily available but also to maintain digital copies of your degrees, certificates, and other pertinent materials such as projects, documents, and writings that can be utilized throughout the application process.  Save them in PDF format as that is the most commonly accepted form of upload.

## Some Final Words of Advice

Preparing your resume and cover letter is a crucial step in the job application process. Here are some reminders of what to keep in mind while working on them both.

1. **Tailor Each Application:** Customize your resume and cover letter for each job you apply to. Highlight relevant skills, experiences, and qualifications that match the specific job requirements. Employers appreciate candidates who show they've done their homework.

2. **Clear and Concise:** Keep your resume and cover letter concise and easy to read. Use bullet points and short, impactful sentences to convey information. Avoid jargon or overly technical language unless it's essential for the position.

3. **Highlight Achievements:** Instead of just listing job duties, focus on your accomplishments and contributions in previous roles. Use quantifiable metrics whenever possible to demonstrate your impact. For example, mention how you increased sales by a certain percentage or completed a project ahead of schedule.

4. **Showcase Transferable Skills:** If you're changing careers or industries, emphasize transferable skills that are relevant to the new role. Explain how your previous experiences have equipped you with the abilities needed for the job you're applying for.

5. **Professional Formatting:** Ensure your resume and cover letter are well-formatted and free of errors. Use a clean, professional font and maintain consistent formatting throughout. Proofread carefully or consider using a tool like Grammarly to catch any grammatical or spelling mistakes.

6. **Focus on the Cover Letter:** Your cover letter should complement your resume by providing context and a narrative. Explain why you're interested in the position and the company, and how your skills align with their needs. Use it as an opportunity to demonstrate your enthusiasm and personality.

7. **Avoid Generic Templates:** While templates can be helpful, avoid using generic, cookie-cutter templates that don't stand out. Customize your documents to reflect your unique qualifications and personality.

8. **Quantify Your Achievements:** Whenever possible, quantify your achievements with specific numbers or percentages. This adds credibility to your claims and gives employers a better understanding of your impact.

9. **Use Keywords:** Many companies use applicant tracking systems (ATS) to scan resumes for relevant keywords. Study the job description and incorporate relevant keywords into your resume and cover letter to increase your chances of passing through the ATS.

10. **Seek Feedback:** Before submitting your documents, ask a trusted friend, mentor, or career advisor to review them. They can provide valuable feedback and catch errors you might have missed.

Remember that your resume and cover letter are your first impression on potential employers. Taking the time to create tailored, well-crafted documents can significantly improve your chances of landing interviews and ultimately securing the job you desire.

## 6.5 Conclusion:

Congratulations! You have now mastered the art of resume writing. In this chapter, we explored the purpose of a resume, learned how to structure it in effective ways, and discovered techniques to tailor it for specific job applications. By following the strategies outlined in this chapter, you are now equipped with the tools to create a standout resume that effectively communicates your unique value proposition.

Crafting a successful resume is an ongoing process. As you gain new experiences and skills, revisit and update your resume accordingly. Additionally, seek feedback from mentors, career advisors, or trusted individuals who can provide valuable insights.

Preparing for success in a job is a vital step in achieving your professional goals. By carefully planning and equipping yourself with the necessary tools and skills, you can position yourself for success in landing that first contact and, ultimately, an interview.

# Chapter 7: Mastering the Art of Interviewing

Congratulations! You have successfully built a strong resume, expanded your professional network, and now it's time to take the next step towards landing your dream job. In this chapter, we will delve into the art of interviewing and provide you with some strategies to ace your interviews.

Whether you are a job seeker, a recent graduate, or someone looking to make a career change, mastering the art of interviewing will set you apart from the competition and help you secure the job you've always wanted.

## 7.1 Preparing for Success

Interviewers often ask a set of common questions to assess candidates' qualifications and fit. Some questions are generic and geared to most applicants, no matter the field or position. Other questions are geared to understanding the technical knowledge of the candidate for that position. The internet provides a cornucopia of interview questions for all candidates of all backgrounds and professions. Take full advantage of that resource to empower yourself with confidence.

Review the questions. Write pertinent ones down and prepare short and concise answers and practice answering them without looking at your written answers. By practicing your answers, you will feel confident and prepared during the interview.

Remember:
- Research the company and the role you're applying for and be prepared to discuss your skills and experiences based on company notes.
- Practice common interview questions.
- Showcase your enthusiasm, demonstrate your knowledge about the company, and ask insightful questions during interviews.
- Prepare examples of your accomplishments and be ready to articulate how your skills align with the job requirements.
- Prepare. Practice. Then prepare and practice again.

In the interview process, while interviewers primarily focus on assessing your job-related qualifications, they also seek to understand your personality and how well you would fit into their team. The key to success lies in being true to yourself and presenting your genuine qualities. So, try to remain relaxed and approach the interview as a friendly conversation where you can openly share all your strengths and abilities.

Let's get started on building your interviewing skills and rapport with future employers.

### 7.1.1 Researching the Company and Position

Thoroughly researching the company and the position you are applying for is crucial for interview success. Research the company to understand their values, mission, and culture. See who's on the Board of Directors or who's who there. If there are blogs, read a few of the latest articles or check out if they've done anything on YouTube or Facebook or other social media to arm yourself with topics that you can bring up at the interview as part of the conversation.

Another crucial step is to **learn how to align your skills and experiences with the job requirements**, so you can show a prospective employer how you will fit into their role. Use things you've learned during your research to relate to while discussing your own accomplishments. Tie it in and show them you have what it takes to be a part of that company and culture.

> Research prospective employers on company review platforms like Glassdoor or Indeed Company Reviews. Gain insights into company culture, employee experiences, and salary information. Reviews from current and former employees can help you make informed decisions and prepare for interviews with specific companies.

Once you have a good idea of the company you are applying for, you want to master your interviewing skills.

## 7.1.2 Mastering Common Interview Questions

Mastering interview skills and techniques is essential for job seekers to enhance their prospects of success. While the topic is extensive, the following is a brief list of ideas for you to consider and make use of. Engaging in mock interviews with friends, colleagues, or seeking assistance from teachers or industry leaders can greatly contribute to improving your skills. It is remarkable how many individuals are willing to support others in achieving success. This is where your networking skills will be put to the test and can come in very handy to achieving your success!

Remember, mastering interview skills is an ongoing process, and practice is key. By preparing thoroughly, showcasing your strengths, and actively engaging in the interview process, you can greatly increase your chances of success.

Practical Exercise with Examples:
The internet is full of helpful resources when it comes to finding interview questions. There are generic interview questions as well as industry type questions. You don't have to know everything but having an idea of the types of questions that may be asked of you will help you to increase your confidence level. Prepare valid answers that are short and concise. Be honest and use your own words so that it's easier for you convey your own thoughts to the interviewer.

- What makes you unique?
- Tell me about yourself and your qualifications.
- Why do you want to work at this company?
- What interests you about this role?
- What motivates you?
- What are your greatest strengths?

- What are your greatest weaknesses?
- What are your goals for the future?
- Where do you think you'll be in five years?
- What did you like most about your last position?
- What did you like least about your last position?
- Can you tell me about a difficult work situation and how you overcame it?
- How do you respond to stress or change?
- How do you handle conflict at work?
- What is your greatest accomplishment?
- How do you define success?
- How do your skills align with this role?
- Why should we hire you?
- Why are you leaving your current job?
- What is your salary range expectation?
- Do you have any questions?
- What are you passionate about?
- What is your teaching philosophy?
- What does customer service mean to you?
- Tell me about your work experience?
- How do you work under pressure?
- What is your dream job?
- What can you bring to the company?

Reference: https://www.indeed.com/career-advice/interviewing/top-interview-questions-and-answers

Practical Examples:
Here are a few sites that can help you get started on preparing some interview questions.

https://emeritus.org/in/learn/common-it-interview-questions-and-answers/
https://www.themuse.com/advice/51-interview-questions-you-should-be-asking

There are many resources that are tailored to specific professions. Your most effective approach is to conduct a Google search using the query "interview questions for xyz" to explore the links Google generates. Additionally, you can rely on ChatGPT to request valid interview questions. Furthermore, scrutinizing the job description itself can provide insight into particular questions that might arise, especially if the role necessitates discussing specific skills.

Questions for the Interviewer
One of the questions that often gets overlooked but one where you should be prepared to answer is, "Do you have any questions for us?". Even if you feel you may not have any questions, you should still go ahead and prepare a few to ask the interviewer. This will show the initiative on your part that you truly are interested in working there.

Here are some questions you might want to ask.

- Ask about the team you'll be working with. How big is it. Where are they located.
- Ask how long the interviewer has been at the company and what they think are the plus points of working there.
- Ask about an HR benefit that you weren't too sure about such as work hours.
- Ask about what goals should look like for you in six months or in a year. Or ask what the first weeks might look like for you and what expectations they would like to have.
- Ask them about the types of projects you might be working on the day you start.
- Ask them what resources they would recommend learning more about a skill that they listed which you may have some knowledge of but would help you to be more prepared on.

The questions you want to ask are to learn a little more about the company and to learn a little more about your future in relation to the position. Don't be shy to ask questions you may think are irrelevant. **The difference between landing a job and being passed over could depend on your own inquisitiveness.**

Harvard Business Review has quite a variety of questions one can ask a prospective interviewer.

[Reference: https://hbr.org/2022/05/38-smart-questions-to-ask-in-a-job-interview ]

### 7.1.3 Develop Your Unique Selling Proposition (USP)

Differentiating yourself from other candidates is key to standing out during interviews. In chapter 1.2 we went over the specific points to cover for your personal USP. You should make every effort to remember to mention all six selling points using real and tangible examples: Leadership, Problem-solving, Communication, Adaptable, Cross-cultural Competence and Innovativeness.

Practice your USPs so that you can effectively communicate them to your interviewers and make a lasting impression.

Practical Exercise:
If you have not done so already, create your USP list and practice repeating them without looking at your notes.

### 7.2 Mastering Interview Techniques

Mastering interview techniques is essential for job seekers aiming to stand out and increase their chances of success. By mastering interview techniques, you can effectively showcase your qualifications, connect with interviewers, and leave a lasting positive impression.

Perfecting interviewing skills is an art that involves a combination of preparation, practice, and adaptability. It's not just about having the right answers; it's also about effectively communicating your qualifications, demonstrating your personality, and building a connection with the interviewer.

Here are a few key points to consider.

1. **Research**: Thoroughly research the company, its culture, values, products/services, and recent developments. This knowledge not only helps you answer questions more effectively but also shows your genuine interest.

2. **Self-Assessment**: Understand your strengths, weaknesses, and unique selling points. Be ready to discuss specific examples from your experiences that highlight these attributes.

3. **STAR Method**: When answering behavioral questions, use the STAR method (Situation, Task, Action, Result) to provide structured and comprehensive responses that showcase your skills and accomplishments.

4. **Tailor Responses**: Customize your responses to align with the specific role you're applying for. Highlight experiences that demonstrate your fitness for the position.

5. **Practice Responses**: Anticipate common interview questions and practice your answers. Rehearsing helps you articulate your thoughts more clearly and confidently.

6. **Not Knowing Something**: Learn how to say that you may not know something fully but have the skills to pick it up quickly. Or you can relate a prior experience to illustrate that you have some familiarity with the subject matter, albeit not to the extent necessary for the current position. This demonstrates your ability to identify analogous skills that can subsequently be enhanced.

7. **Nonverbal Communication**: Pay attention to your body language, eye contact, and tone of voice. Project confidence, professionalism, and enthusiasm through your nonverbal cues.

8. **Ask Thoughtful Questions**: Prepare questions that demonstrate your interest in the company and role. Inquire about the team, expectations, growth opportunities, and company culture.

9. **Mock Interviews**: Conduct mock interviews with a friend, family member, or career coach. Constructive feedback can help you refine your responses and improve your overall performance.

10. **Time Management**: Be mindful of your response length. Aim for concise yet informative answers to avoid rambling or going off-topic.

11. **Adaptability**: Be ready to think on your feet. Sometimes, interviewers might ask unexpected questions to gauge your problem-solving abilities and adaptability.

12. **Follow-Up**: Send a thank-you email after the interview, expressing gratitude for the opportunity and reiterating your interest in the role.

13. **Reflect and Learn**: After each interview, reflect on what went well and what could be improved. Learning from each experience enhances your skills for future interviews.

It benefits to say again that interviewing is a skill that improves with time and effort. Each interview is a chance to refine your approach and build confidence in presenting yourself effectively to potential employers.

### 7.2.1 Perfecting Your Nonverbal Communication
The impact of nonverbal cues on interview success cannot be understated. Although a vast subject in its own right, it's crucial to bear in mind that your appearance and demeanor will leave a lasting impression on your interviewer. Frequently, words may fade from memory, but a gesture or expression can linger in their thoughts.

It's imperative to be mindful of your body language, facial cues, and tone of voice throughout the interview process. Demonstrating self-assuredness, sustaining meaningful eye contact, and exhibiting active listening all contribute to projecting confidence.

Your nonverbal presentation significantly contributes to forging a connection with the interviewer, showcasing your professionalism.

Practical Exercise:
While it might initially seem unconventional, practicing in front of a mirror can be a valuable tool for self-assessment of your reactions and body language. Consider rehearsing your interview skills while seated in front of a standing mirror, as it provides an optimal view of your hand gestures, posture, and any excessive fidgeting. The more you practice, the more adept you become at confronting and addressing your fears and nervous habits.

### 7.2.2 Answering Behavioral Interview Questions
Carefully designed, behavioral interview questions are aimed at exploring your past actions to assess your potential for future success. Strive to present a genuine and vibrant depiction, vividly showcasing how you would skillfully navigate a specific scenario. It's important to be candid and draw from your own personal encounters. Remember, there isn't a flawless response, but your goal is to demonstrate how you can remain composed, astute, and modest in the face of any challenge.

### 7.2.3 The STAR Method
The STAR method is a structured approach used to answer behavioral interview questions by providing clear and concise responses that highlight your experiences and skills. It stands for Situation, Task, Action, and Result, and it helps you deliver a comprehensive and organized answer.

Here's a breakdown of each component.

1. **Situation**: Begin by describing the situation or context in which the experience you're discussing took place. Set the stage by providing relevant details, such as the company, the project, or the challenge you faced. This helps the interviewer understand the scenario.

2. **Task**: Clearly outline the task or objective you were assigned or that arose from the situation. What goal were you trying to achieve, or problem were you aiming to solve? This step helps the interviewer understand the purpose of your actions.

3. **Action**: Describe the specific actions you took to address the situation or task. Highlight your role, responsibilities, and the steps you followed. Focus on your contributions and the skills you employed. This is where you demonstrate your abilities and expertise.

4. **Result**: Explain the outcomes of your actions. What were the quantifiable or qualitative results of your efforts? Did you achieve the desired outcome, and if so, how did it impact the situation or task? This demonstrates the effectiveness of your actions and provides a tangible example of your capabilities.

Using the STAR method, your response becomes a well-structured narrative that showcases your abilities and experiences in a coherent manner. This method is particularly effective for answering questions that start with phrases like "Tell me about a time when..." or "Give me an example of..." It helps interviewers understand how you approach challenges, make decisions, and contribute to your team or organization.

Here's a simplified example using the STAR method:

**Question**: "Tell me about a time when you had to work under a tight deadline."

**Situation**: At my previous job as a marketing coordinator, we were assigned a last-minute project to create a presentation for an important client meeting.

**Task**: The task was to gather all the necessary information, design the presentation, and finalize it within 24 hours.

**Action**: I immediately assembled a small team, dividing the tasks among us. I gathered relevant data, created a detailed outline, and delegated sections to team members based on their strengths. We worked collaboratively and efficiently, communicating updates to ensure everyone was aligned.

**Result**: Despite the time constraint, we successfully completed the presentation ahead of the deadline. The client was impressed with the quality and timeliness of our work, which led to positive feedback from our manager and an increased sense of teamwork within the department.

**Using the STAR method, your answers become more structured, focused, and impactful, allowing you to effectively demonstrate your skills and experiences to potential employers.**

### 7.2.4 Handling Challenging Interview Situations
In interviews, it's quite typical to face demanding circumstances, such as challenging questions or unforeseen scenarios. While most interviewers do not intentionally aim to unsettle a prospective employee with unexpected queries or situations, it's possible that they might inquire about

something that takes you by surprise. In such situations, it's essential to remain composed. Your prior experiences and the effort you've put into researching the company's mission and culture will enable you to provide a well-thought-out response without appearing startled or perplexed.

Here are some real examples illustrating how you can navigate through these situations with grace and confidence.

1. **Navigating Tricky Questions**:
   Example: If asked about a past failure or mistake, instead of getting defensive, you can acknowledge the situation, take responsibility, and highlight the lessons learned. This showcases your ability to reflect, grow, and use setbacks as opportunities for improvement.

2. **Addressing Gaps in Experience**:
   Example: If you lack experience in a particular area relevant to the job, you can highlight transferable skills or related experiences that demonstrate your ability to quickly learn and adapt. Emphasize your enthusiasm and eagerness to acquire new knowledge and skills.

3. **Turning Weaknesses into Strengths**:
   Example: When discussing a potential weakness, you can focus on how you have actively worked to overcome it. For instance, if you struggled with public speaking, you could mention joining a Toastmasters club or taking communication courses to improve your skills. This demonstrates your determination, growth mindset, and willingness to invest in self-improvement.

4. **Handling Unexpected Scenarios**:
   Example: During a case study or problem-solving exercise, if faced with an unexpected twist or challenging constraint, maintain composure, and think critically. Communicate your thought process, break down the problem into manageable parts, and propose logical solutions. This showcases your adaptability, analytical thinking, and ability to perform under pressure.

By equipping yourself with these strategies, you can confidently navigate challenging situations in interviews. Remember, practice and preparation play a significant role in building your confidence and ability to handle unexpected scenarios.

Practical Exercise:
Using some of the questions you saw earlier in section 7.1.2, try to create answers using the STAR method.

## 7.3 Compensation

Salary discussions can be sensitive and require careful handling, but it is crucial to address them effectively to ensure fair compensation. The following examples can help you in navigating this process by providing strategies for researching salary benchmarks, understanding your own value, and effectively negotiating your desired compensation package.

1. **Researching Salary Benchmarks**:

    Example: Before entering salary discussions, it is important to research industry standards and salary ranges for similar roles in your geographic location. Utilize reliable salary surveys, online resources, and professional networks to gather information. This research will provide you with a solid foundation to evaluate and negotiate your worth.

2. **Understanding Your Worth**:

    Example: Assess your skills, experience, qualifications, and unique value proposition. Consider your past achievements, level of expertise, and any specialized knowledge you bring to the role. By recognizing your worth, you can confidently articulate your value to potential employers and demonstrate why you deserve fair compensation.

3. **Discussing Salary Expectations**:

    Example: When discussing salary expectations, it is crucial to strike a balance between expressing your value and remaining flexible. Clearly communicate your desired salary range based on your research and market value. Emphasize the value you bring to the organization and the impact you can make. Remain open to a constructive dialogue to explore other aspects of the compensation package, such as benefits, bonuses, or professional development opportunities.

4. **Negotiating a Fair Compensation Package**:

    Example: During negotiations, maintain a professional and collaborative approach. Focus on the overall value proposition rather than just the base salary. Discuss additional factors that are important to you, such as work-life balance, career growth opportunities, or flexibility. Consider creative solutions, such as performance-based incentives or milestone-driven salary increases, to align your compensation with your contributions and future potential.

5. **Handling Counteroffers**:

    Example: If you receive a counteroffer from your current employer or another company, carefully evaluate the complete package, including salary, benefits, and growth opportunities. Assess whether the offer aligns with your career goals and long-term aspirations. When making decisions, consider the overall fit, organizational culture, and the potential for professional growth.

By keeping these points in mind, you can approach salary discussions with confidence and negotiate a fair compensation package that aligns with your worth and the value you bring to the table.

Remember to maintain professionalism, conduct thorough research, and be open to a constructive dialogue that benefits both you and the employer.

## 7.4 The "Thank You" Letter

After submitting your applications and attending interviews, it is essential to follow up with a personalized message or thank-you note to express your appreciation. This gesture demonstrates professionalism, gratitude, and a genuine interest in the position.
Here are a few key points to consider when writing your Thank You letter.

1. **Timeliness**:
   Send your follow-up message or thank-you note within 24 to 48 hours of the interview or application submission. This ensures that it remains fresh in the recipient's mind and showcases your promptness.

2. **Personalization**:
   Tailor your message to the specific individual or individuals you interacted with during the application process or interview. Mention specific points from your conversation or the application process to show that you were actively engaged and attentive.

3. **Express gratitude**:
   Begin your message by expressing gratitude for the opportunity to apply or interview for the position. Acknowledge the time and effort the interviewer or hiring team invested in considering your application or conducting the interview.

4. **Reflect on the experience**:
   Briefly mention the positive aspects of the interview or application process and how it reinforced your interest in the position or the company. Highlight any key insights or takeaways you gained from the experience.

5. **Reiterate your qualifications**:
   Take the opportunity to reaffirm your skills, experiences, and unique qualities that make you a strong fit for the role. Emphasize how your qualifications align with the company's needs and showcase your enthusiasm for contributing to their success.

6. **Personal touch**:
   Add a personalized touch to your message. For example, if you discussed a shared interest or had a memorable moment during the interview, briefly mention it to help you stand out and create a connection.

7. **Professional tone**:
   Keep the tone of your message professional and courteous. Avoid any negative or overly casual language and focus on conveying your appreciation and interest in the position.

8. **Proofread before sending**:

> Before hitting the send button, carefully proofread your message to ensure it is error-free, concise, and well-structured. A polished and well-written follow-up message or thank-you note reflects positively on your attention to detail and communication skills.

Remember, **a well-crafted follow-up message or thank-you note can leave a lasting impression and set you apart from other candidates**. It demonstrates your professionalism, gratitude, and interest in the opportunity, and can potentially influence the decision-making process in your favor.

> When composing your email to them, ensure to highlight your unique selling proposition (USP). By refreshing a prospective manager's memory about your distinctive skills, experiences, and personal qualities that set you apart, you can make a lasting impression regarding the unique value you bring, which others may have overlooked mentioning.

Practical Exercise:
Create a template for a Thank You letter that you can modify with job specific notes, as needed.

## 7.5 Conclusion:

By preparing thoroughly, mastering interview techniques, and effectively showcasing your value, you will leave a lasting impression on interviewers and increase your chances of success.

Remember, interviews are not only an opportunity for employers to evaluate you but also for you to assess whether the company aligns with your career goals and values. Approach interviews with confidence, authenticity, and a genuine curiosity to learn more about the company.

# Chapter 8: The Path to Continuous Growth and Professional Development

By now, you have learned valuable strategies for personal growth, networking, interviewing to help you land your dream job. But the journey doesn't end once you have landed the job. In Chapter 8, we will explore the importance of continuous growth and professional development to ensure long-term success in your chosen career path.

In today's rapidly evolving job market, having a growth mindset is crucial to adapt to change, embrace challenges, and unlock your full potential. **Building a fulfilling and prosperous career requires continuous growth, adaptability, and a proactive mindset**.

It is important to emphasize the significance of lifelong learning for career success. You need to stay curious about your field of work, embracing new technologies and trends, and seeking out opportunities for professional development. You will need to cultivate a growth mindset and integrate learning into your daily routine. Nurturing a mindset primed for growth and seamlessly weaving learning into your everyday activities becomes imperative. This process of learning extends beyond the conventional trajectory embraced by others, encompassing the uncharted paths that can usher in fresh viewpoints and novel perspectives.

This chapter discusses some of the ways you can navigate the ever-evolving professional landscape and thrive in your chosen field. You will need to have a positive mindset, be resilient and adaptable, and know how to learn from setbacks and failures. By cultivating a growth mindset, you can navigate the complexities of your career journey and find a better job that aligns with your aspirations.

## 8.1 Embracing a Growth Mindset

A growth mindset is the belief that your abilities can be developed through dedication and hard work. It requires you to embrace the positive side of all that you've done and accomplished and use any failures as learning points. Failures should not define you but rather help you to see where you need further help and improvements on.

### 8.1.1 The Power of a Growth Mindset

Your mindset plays a significant role in shaping your career trajectory. Embracing a positive mindset can unlock doors of opportunity and pave the way for personal and professional growth.

Here are some key elements to consider.

1. **The power of positivity**:

   Positivity fuels motivation, creativity, and resilience. It allows you to approach challenges with a can-do attitude and see setbacks as steppingstones to success. Cultivate a positive outlook by practicing gratitude, surrounding yourself with supportive individuals, and embracing a growth mindset.

2. **Self-belief and confidence**:

> Believe in your abilities and have confidence in your potential. Recognize your strengths and accomplishments and use them as pillars of self-assurance. When you believe in yourself, you exude confidence, making you more attractive to potential employers and increasing your chances of finding a better job.

3. **Self-talk and affirmations**:

> Pay attention to your inner dialogue. Replace negative self-talk with positive affirmations that reinforce your capabilities and potential. Affirmations can boost your confidence, rewire your mindset, and propel you towards career success.

4. **Continuous learning and improvement**:

> Adopt a mindset of continuous learning. Embrace opportunities to acquire new skills, expand your knowledge, and stay abreast of industry trends. A growth mindset embraces challenges as opportunities for growth and is eager to acquire new knowledge to stay competitive in the job market.

5. **Failures are opportunities to improve**:

> View failures as opportunities for learning and improvement in those things that you may not be strong at. This self-realization can help to guide you to learning things in a new way that applies to your desired roles.

## 8.1.2 Setting Meaningful Goals

Goal setting is essential for personal and professional growth. We will guide you through the process of setting SMART goals—Specific, Measurable, Achievable, Relevant, and Time-bound. By setting meaningful goals, you will learn how to align your goals with your long-term vision and break them down into actionable steps for success.

Set goals for personal skill development.

- Based on your self-evaluation and the skills you want to improve on, set specific and achievable goals.
- Break down your goals into actionable steps and create a timeline for completion.
- Identify resources or learning opportunities that can help you develop those skills (e.g., courses, workshops, mentors).
- Continue to revise your skillset in other topics if you plan to transition to something different later in your career path.

## 8.1.3 Cultivating Resiliency and Adaptability

Resilience and adaptability stand as critical attributes for achieving career success in the ever-evolving job market of today. Devoid of these qualities, you risk becoming stagnant in your professional journey. While it may not always be feasible to switch gears instantaneously, it is imperative to effectively embrace changes in a deliberate and pragmatic manner. Achieving this necessitates a shift in mindset that enables personal growth. This entails setting aside any ego or pride associated with your current status and prioritizing your ultimate goals over your present circumstances.

Here are some ways you can cultivate these traits.

1. **Embrace change**:
   > Rather than fearing change, view it as an opportunity for growth. Embrace new technologies, industry shifts, and evolving job market demands. Be open to acquiring new skills and adapting to new ways of working.

2. **Develop problem-solving skills**:
   > Challenges are inevitable in any career. Cultivate your problem-solving skills by breaking down complex problems, seeking creative solutions, and remaining calm under pressure. Embrace challenges as opportunities to showcase your adaptability and resilience.

3. **Seek feedback and learn from it:**
   > Constructive feedback provides valuable insights for growth. Embrace feedback as a means to improve and learn from your experiences. Actively seek feedback from mentors, colleagues, and employers, and use it to refine your skills and enhance your performance.

4. **Build a support network:**
   > Surround yourself with a supportive network of individuals who uplift and encourage you. Seek mentors who have navigated similar career paths and can provide guidance and support. Your support network can help you stay resilient and navigate challenges with confidence.

Remember that being resilient and adaptable broadens your horizons and does not limit the range of job opportunities you can explore.

## 8.1.4 Learning from Setbacks and Failures

Setbacks and failures are natural parts of any career journey. Learning from these experiences can fuel personal growth and lead you to better opportunities.

Here are some ways you can approach setbacks and failures with a growth mindset in place.

1. **Embrace a growth-oriented perspective**:
   > Rather than viewing setbacks as failures, see them as learning opportunities. Embrace a growth-oriented perspective that focuses on continuous improvement and resilience. Reflect on your setbacks, identify lessons learned, and apply them to future endeavors.

2. **Analyze and adapt**:
   > When faced with a setback, take a step back and analyze the situation objectively. Identify the factors that contributed to the setback and develop a plan to overcome them. Adjust your strategies, learn from the experience, and move forward with renewed determination.

3. **Develop resilience**:
   > Resilience is the ability to bounce back from adversity. Cultivate resilience by maintaining a positive outlook, staying motivated, and seeking support when needed. Remember, setbacks

are temporary, and with resilience, you can overcome them and continue your journey towards finding a better job.

**4. Practice self-compassion:**

Be kind to yourself when faced with setbacks or failures. Treat yourself with the same compassion and understanding you would offer to a friend. Acknowledge that setbacks are part of the learning process and use them as opportunities for growth and improvement.

**Never let failure be an option.** It can happen, but it does not need to be the determining factor for what you do next in your professional or personal growth.

## 8.1.5 Overcoming Imposter Syndrome

Imposter syndrome is a common phenomenon that can hinder your progress and confidence. We will discuss strategies for overcoming imposter syndrome, including reframing negative self-talk, celebrating your achievements, and seeking support from mentors and peers. By acknowledging your worth and embracing your capabilities, you will overcome self-doubt and thrive in your career.

## 8.2 Developing Key Skills

Throughout your career, it is imperative that you develop some essential key skills that have universal applicability across various industries. Communication skills, leadership capabilities and effectively managing time are extremely important regardless of your chosen career path. While this topic encompasses a wide range of considerations, we'll outline some key factors to bear in mind.

## 8.2.1 Enhancing Communication Skills

Effective communication is crucial in every professional setting. It is important to improve your verbal and written communication skills, your ability to actively listen to your audience, and know how to resolve conflicts. You need to learn how to convey your ideas clearly, collaborate effectively, and build strong relationships with colleagues and stakeholders.

Even if English isn't your native language, it remains essential to learn how to effectively convey your ideas and thoughts to your audience. This is where dedicated practice becomes crucial, whether it involves rehearsing in front of a mirror or engaging with individuals in your professional network. Enhancing your communication skills is vital, as it enables you to bridge language barriers and connect with others in various contexts.

For instance, if you're not a native English speaker, you might practice your pronunciation and enunciation by reading aloud and recording yourself. Sharing these recordings with friends, colleagues, or language exchange partners can provide valuable feedback on your clarity and fluency. Additionally, participating in public speaking clubs or workshops can help refine your communication abilities, regardless of your language background.

**Ultimately, the ability to effectively convey your ideas transcends language fluency and is a valuable asset in any career.**

### 8.2.2 Sharpening Leadership Abilities

Leadership skills are valuable regardless of your job title. It is important to learn what are the essential qualities of a successful leader and provide strategies for developing your own leadership abilities. You will need to learn how to inspire and motivate others, delegate tasks, and navigate challenging situations with grace and empathy.

There's a common misconception that leadership skills are exclusively relevant to individuals in managerial roles or those aspiring to manage others. However, this is far from accurate. Leadership skills hold significance at every stage of a person's professional journey. They serve as valuable tools not only for those in managerial positions but also for individuals in various roles and levels within an organization.

Leadership skills offer guidance in addressing personal conflicts within a team, fostering collaboration, and nurturing effective decision-making. For example, if you're working in a non-managerial role, demonstrating leadership skills might involve taking initiative, showing accountability, and influencing positive outcomes within your team. By facilitating productive discussions, motivating colleagues, and being a reliable team player, you exhibit leadership qualities that contribute to the success of your group and, ultimately, your career progression.

In essence, **leadership skills are versatile assets that benefit individuals across all career stages and roles**, as they empower individuals to excel both as team members and potential leaders in their own right.

### 8.2.3 Mastering Time Management

Effective time management plays a pivotal role in sustaining productivity and attaining your objectives. It entails mastering the art of task prioritization, adeptly navigating deadlines, and steering clear of the usual time-draining pitfalls. To excel in this skill, you must become proficient in crafting well-structured schedules, eliminating distractions, and harnessing your productivity to its fullest potential.

For instance, prioritization involves identifying tasks that are most critical to your goals and tackling them first. By doing so, you ensure that essential projects receive the attention they deserve, leading to better outcomes. Additionally, mastering the creation of efficient schedules aids in optimizing your daily routine, allowing for a well-balanced allocation of your time and energy.

Moreover, eliminating distractions, such as silencing notifications during work hours or organizing your workspace for maximum focus, contributes significantly to enhanced time management. By managing your time effectively, you not only boost productivity but also create space for personal growth and work-life balance.

## 8.3 Embracing Lifelong Learning

Regardless of your chosen profession, continuous learning should be a fundamental aspect of your life. It extends beyond professional advancement, encompassing the acquisition of personal knowledge and accomplishments. The opportunities for learning are boundless, and they exist without regard to time constraints.

For instance, a software engineer may engage in ongoing learning to keep up with evolving programming languages and technologies, enhancing their professional skills. Simultaneously, they might pursue personal interests like learning to play a musical instrument, a non-professional endeavor that contributes to their overall growth and fulfillment.

**The quest for knowledge and skill development knows no bounds and can be pursued at any stage of life.**

### 8.3.1 Seeking Professional Development Opportunities

Continuing education and professional development are essential for staying ahead in your career. We should explore various avenues for professional development, including workshops, online courses, conferences, and industry certifications. You will need to learn how to identify relevant opportunities and invest in your growth so that you are never too far behind the times.

But before we can go down the path of how to improve your skills, you must first identify what you want to improve.

1. Identify skills you want to develop or improve:
    - What skills do you currently lack or want to enhance?
    - Are there any areas where you feel you have untapped potential?
    - How would improving these skills benefit your personal or professional growth?

2. Seek feedback from others:
    - Talk to trusted colleagues, supervisors, or mentors about your skills.
    - Request constructive feedback on your strengths and areas for improvement.
    - Consider their perspectives and insights to gain a well-rounded view of your abilities.

Practical Exercise:
Using some of what you delved into in section 1.1, start making a list of skills and knowledge that you would like to add to your professional toolbelt.

### 8.3.2 Identifying Skill Gaps and Pursuing Learning Opportunities

Identifying skill gaps is essential for personal and professional development. Here are some ways you can identify skill gaps and strategies to fill them:

1. **Self-assessment**:

    Reflect on your current skills and knowledge. Evaluate your strengths and weaknesses in relation to your goals. Consider the skills required in your field or industry and compare them to your existing skill set. Identify areas where you feel less confident or lack proficiency.

## 2. Seek feedback:

Request feedback from supervisors, colleagues, or mentors. They can provide insights into areas where you can improve and identify skill gaps you may not have noticed. Their perspective can help you gain a more accurate understanding of your strengths and weaknesses.

## 3. Conduct a SWOT analysis:

Perform a SWOT (**Strengths, Weaknesses, Opportunities, Threats**) analysis on yourself. This analysis involves identifying your strengths and weaknesses (skill gaps) and assessing the opportunities and threats related to your goals. It helps you gain a comprehensive overview of areas that need improvement.

## 4. Stay updated with industry trends:

Follow industry publications, websites, blogs, and social media channels to stay informed about the latest trends, advancements, and skills demanded in your field. This can help you identify emerging skills that may be valuable in your career.

## 5. Benchmark against job descriptions:

Review job descriptions or roles you aspire to. Note the required skills and qualifications. Compare your current skill set to the desired skills mentioned in those descriptions. Identify gaps between the job requirements and your current abilities.

## 6. Utilize self-assessment tools:

There are various online self-assessment tools available that can help you identify skill gaps. These tools often involve questionnaires or assessments that evaluate your knowledge and abilities in specific areas. They provide insights into areas where you may need improvement.

## 7. Seek professional development opportunities:

Look for courses, workshops, webinars, or training programs that target the skills you want to develop. Online learning platforms, industry associations, and local educational institutions often offer these opportunities. Enroll in relevant courses to bridge your skill gaps.

## 8. Mentorship and coaching:

Seek guidance from mentors or coaches who have expertise in the areas you want to improve. They can provide personalized advice, suggest resources, and offer support as you work on filling your skill gaps. Their experience can help you navigate the learning process effectively.

## 9. On-the-job learning:

Look for opportunities within your current role or projects that allow you to develop the skills you lack. Take on new responsibilities, volunteer for tasks that require the skills you want to acquire or seek cross-functional projects. Learning by doing can be a powerful way to fill skill gaps.

10. **Networking and collaboration**:

> Engage with professionals who possess the skills you want to develop. Connect with them through networking events, online communities, or industry-specific platforms. Collaborate on projects, seek guidance, or learn from their experiences. Building relationships with skilled individuals can provide learning opportunities and support in skill development.

Remember, filling skill gaps takes time and effort. Be patient, persistent, and consistent in your learning journey. Continuously evaluate your progress and reassess your skill gaps to ensure you are on track. By actively working on filling these gaps, you can enhance your capabilities and advance in your career.

To optimize your learning journey, it is vital to create a well-organized learning plan. Begin by identifying the specific skills you wish to acquire or improve. Next, explore various online resources such as free courses, educational videos on platforms like YouTube, paid courses, seminars, educational institutions, and mentorship programs that offer relevant training. Some of these opportunities may even provide professional certifications to enhance your credentials.

Practical Exercise:
Using the list you created in 8.3.1, add more detail on where you can acquire said skills. Set a plan on how you can achieve said skills.  Print it out and put it someplace near you as a reminder that you have work to do.

## 8.3.3 Building a Personal Learning Network

Building a personal learning network (PLN) involves connecting with professionals who share your interests and goals, and who can provide support, knowledge, and resources to enhance your learning and growth.

Here are some steps to help you build a PLN for yourself.

1. **Identify your interests and goals:**

> Determine the areas of knowledge or skills you want to develop. Clarify your learning objectives and what you hope to achieve through your PLN. This will help you focus on finding professionals who align with your interests.

2. **Engage in professional communities:**

> Join online platforms, forums, and social media groups related to your field or area of interest. Actively participate in discussions, ask questions, and share your insights. LinkedIn, Twitter, Facbook groups, and specialized online communities such as Reddit or Stack Exchange are great places to connect with professionals.

3. **Attend conferences and events:**

> Attend industry conferences, seminars, workshops, or local meetups. These events provide opportunities to network with professionals, gain new insights, and discover potential PLN

members. Engage in conversations, exchange contact information, and follow up with individuals you connect with.

### 4. Seek out mentors and experts:

Identify professionals who have expertise in areas you want to explore. Reach out to them with specific questions or requests for advice. Building relationships with mentors and experts can provide valuable guidance and support in your learning journey.

### 5. Participate in online courses or webinars:

Join online courses, webinars, or virtual workshops led by industry experts. These platforms often foster communities where participants can connect, share insights, and support one another's learning. Engage with other learners and instructors to expand your network.

### 6. Utilize social media:

Leverage social media platforms like LinkedIn, Twitter, or Instagram to connect with professionals in your field. Follow thought leaders, influencers, and experts who regularly share valuable content. Engage with their posts, share your thoughts, and build relationships with like-minded individuals.

### 7. Join professional associations or organizations:

Become a member of professional associations or organizations that align with your interests. Attend their events, conferences, or workshops to connect with professionals who are passionate about the same field as you. These associations often provide networking opportunities and access to resources that can support your learning.

### 8. Contribute and share your expertise:

Building a PLN is a two-way street. Share your knowledge, insights, and resources with others. Contribute to discussions, write blog posts, or create content that demonstrates your expertise. By actively participating and offering value to others, you can attract like-minded professionals to your network.

Examples of building a PLN:
- Joining a LinkedIn group dedicated to your industry and actively engaging in discussions and knowledge sharing.
- Attending an industry conference and networking with professionals who share similar interests.
- Participating in an online course or webinar and connecting with fellow learners through discussion forums or virtual study groups.
- Seeking out a mentor in your field and establishing a regular communication channel for guidance and support.
- Joining a professional association related to your career path and attending their events or workshops to meet professionals in your industry.

Remember, building a PLN takes time and effort. Be proactive in reaching out, maintaining relationships, and actively participating in relevant communities. By nurturing your PLN, you can create a supportive network that facilitates continuous learning and growth in your professional journey.

### 8.3.4 Embracing New Technologies and Trends

Technology is rapidly shaping the professional landscape. From learning to perfecting resumes to perfecting the interview, there is no shortage of tools available on the internet. Don't be afraid to search for what you need and use it for personal and professional growth.

> Take advantage of online learning platforms such as Coursera, Udemy, or LinkedIn Learning to enhance your skills and knowledge. Once you have identified areas where you need improvement or want to gain new expertise relevant to your target job roles, find the relevant courses to brush up your skills. Acquiring additional certifications or completing relevant courses can make you a more attractive candidate to employers and shows that you are looking to improve and stay updated on current trends and technologies.

### 8.3.5 Balancing Work and Learning

Juggling work responsibilities and ongoing learning can be a challenging task, but with proper planning and organization, it is achievable.

Here are some initial steps you should take to balance work and learning.

1. **Set clear goals:**
   Define your objectives for both work and learning. Identify what you want to achieve in your career and the specific areas of knowledge you want to develop. Having clear goals will help you prioritize your time and efforts effectively.

2. **Plan and manage your time:**
   Create a schedule that allocates dedicated time for work and learning. Set aside specific blocks of time for focused work and establish regular study periods. Use time management techniques such as the Pomodoro Technique (working in intervals with short breaks) to enhance productivity.

3. **Prioritize tasks:**
   Determine the most important tasks and responsibilities in your work and learning. Focus on high-priority activities that align with your goals and have the most impact. Learning to prioritize will prevent you from becoming overwhelmed and ensure that you make progress in both areas.

### 4. Take advantage of flexible learning options:

Explore flexible learning opportunities that suit your work schedule. Online courses, webinars, podcasts, or even audiobooks can allow you to learn on the go or during your free time. Look for resources that offer self-paced learning, allowing you to study at your own convenience.

### 5. Leverage your work environment:

Identify opportunities within your work environment to incorporate learning. Seek out projects or tasks that align with your learning goals. Additionally, you can explore if your employer offers any training or professional development programs that you can participate in.

### 6. Break down learning into manageable chunks:

Rather than trying to tackle an entire subject at once, break down your learning into smaller, manageable chunks. Focus on one topic or concept at a time, and gradually build upon your knowledge. This approach will make learning more digestible and easier to integrate into your routine.

### 7. Seek support and collaboration:

Connect with like-minded individuals who share your learning interests. Join study groups, online communities, or professional networks where you can exchange ideas and receive support. Collaborating with others can enhance your learning experience and provide valuable insights.

### 8. Maintain a healthy work-life balance:

It's crucial to prioritize self-care and ensure a healthy work-life balance. Set aside time for relaxation, hobbies, and spending time with loved ones. Taking care of your well-being will improve your focus and productivity in both work and learning.

Remember, finding the right balance between work and learning may require experimentation and adjustments. It's important to be flexible and adapt your approach based on your personal circumstances and evolving priorities.

Amidst this journey, always remember to find joy in it. **The path to one's career ambitions often presents obstacles and moments of stress, so it's crucial to prioritize the well-being of your mind, body, and emotions along the way.** While burnout is a possibility, it shouldn't deter you from taking necessary breaks, reevaluating your objectives, and then resuming your personal journey toward success.

Real-Life Examples:
Here are some real-life examples of how someone working a full-time job can balance work and learning:

1. *Utilizing commute time:*
      If you have a long commute, make the most of that time by listening to educational podcasts or audiobooks related to your field of interest. This allows you to continue learning even while traveling to and from work.

2. *Lunchtime learning:*
      Instead of spending your entire lunch break solely on leisure activities, dedicate a portion of that time to learning. You can bring a book or access online learning materials on your phone or laptop to make the most of those brief periods throughout the week.

3. *Negotiating flexible work arrangements:*
      If possible, discuss with your employer the possibility of flexible work arrangements. This could include adjusting your work schedule to have dedicated learning time before or after work hours. Some employers may also offer telecommuting or remote work options, which can provide additional flexibility for learning.

4. *Taking advantage of online courses and webinars:*
      Many reputable online learning platforms offer self-paced courses and webinars that allow you to learn at your own convenience. Take advantage of these resources by allocating specific times during the week to complete coursework or attend live webinars.

5. *Weekend learning sessions:*
      Reserve a few hours over the weekend for focused learning. This can be an opportunity to dive deeper into a subject or work on assignments and projects. By dedicating consistent time each weekend to learning, you can make substantial progress over time.

6. *Maximizing downtime:*
      Identify pockets of time throughout your day where you can fit in short bursts of learning. For example, during your coffee breaks or while waiting for meetings to start, you can read articles or watch educational videos related to your field. These small increments of focused learning can add up over time.

7. *Engaging in professional development opportunities at work:*
      Check if your workplace offers any professional development programs, workshops, or seminars. Attend those that align with your learning goals and can enhance your skills or knowledge in your current role. Some organizations may even provide dedicated work hours for such activities.

Remember, everyone's circumstances and schedules are different, so it's important to find a balance that works best for you. Experiment with different strategies and adapt them to your specific situation to create a sustainable routine for balancing work and learning effectively.

## 8.4 Conclusion:

By implementing the strategies and techniques outlined in this chapter, you will be well-equipped to embark on a lifelong journey of continuous learning and growth.

By embracing a positive mindset, cultivating resilience and adaptability, continued learning, and learning from setbacks and failures, you can navigate your career journey with confidence and find a better job that aligns with your goals and aspirations. Remember, developing a growth mindset is an ongoing process that requires self-reflection, practice, and dedication. Embrace the power of a growth mindset and unlock the doors to a fulfilling and successful career.

Remember, personal growth and professional development are ongoing processes. Embrace a growth mindset, set meaningful goals, and continually enhance your skills. Stay curious, seek new opportunities, and surround yourself with a supportive network of professionals. Remain committed to personal growth, seize opportunities for learning and development, and stay true to your passions and values.

As you navigate your career, remember also that success is not defined by reaching a destination but by the growth and impact you experience along the way. Embrace the challenges, celebrate your achievements, and keep pushing yourself to new heights.

# Chapter 9: Final Words of Encouragement

Congratulations on completing this comprehensive book on personal growth and career success!

Throughout the chapters, we have explored valuable strategies, insights, and tools to empower you on your journey towards finding a better job and achieving long-term career fulfillment.

In today's fast-paced and ever-changing world, it is essential to embrace a proactive mindset and continuously invest in your personal and professional development. By following the actionable steps outlined in this book, you have gained a solid foundation to navigate the challenges and seize the opportunities that lie ahead.

We have emphasized the importance of self-reflection and self-awareness. Understanding your strengths, passions, and values is crucial in making informed career decisions and pursuing opportunities that align with your aspirations. Remember to regularly assess your goals, interests, and growth areas to ensure your career path remains in alignment with your evolving ambitions.

Networking has been identified as a powerful tool for career growth, and we have provided practical tips to help you build and nurture professional relationships. The connections you make along your journey can open doors to new opportunities, provide valuable insights, and support you during career transitions. Remember to approach networking with authenticity, kindness, and a genuine interest in building mutually beneficial connections.

Lifelong learning is an essential aspect of personal growth and career advancement. We discussed the significance of continuous learning, adapting to new technologies and trends, and investing in your professional development. Remember to cultivate a growth mindset, seek out learning opportunities, and stay curious about the latest developments in your field. By embracing lifelong learning, you will remain relevant and resilient in an ever-changing job market.

Achieving sustainable career success also requires maintaining a healthy work-life balance and prioritizing your well-being. It is important that you learn to manage your time effectively, avoiding burnout, and nurturing your physical, mental, and emotional well-being. Remember that success is not solely defined by professional achievements but also by your ability to create a harmonious integration of work and personal life. Prioritize self-care, set boundaries, and engage in activities that bring you joy and fulfillment outside of work.

As you embark on your journey to find a better job and build a fulfilling career, it is essential to stay resilient in the face of challenges and setbacks. Embrace these obstacles as opportunities for growth and learning. Remember that your path may not always be linear, and setbacks are often steppingstones to greater achievements. Stay committed to your goals, stay persistent, and never lose sight of your vision.

Lastly, believe in yourself and your abilities. Confidence is key in pursuing new opportunities and showcasing your unique value to employers. Recognize your accomplishments, celebrate your successes, and use them as fuel to propel you towards even greater achievements.

Thank you for joining us on this transformative journey. We hope this book has provided you with actionable insights, practical strategies, and the inspiration to pursue a career that brings you joy, fulfillment, and financial stability. Remember, the power to find a better job and shape your career lies within you.

Seize the opportunities that come your way, embrace personal growth, and let your passion guide you towards a future filled with success and fulfillment.

Wishing you all the best in your career endeavors. Go forth and thrive!

## Appendix A: Self Evaluation Worksheet

1. Identify your educational background. Outline your educational qualifications and any relevant certifications. Start with the most relevant and the most recent qualification first.

_____
_____
_____
_____
_____

2. What are your top three to five professional achievements or accomplishments?   What roles or positions have you held? What were your responsibilities and duties? What skills did you develop or utilize in those roles? Did you receive any recognition or achieve notable results?

_____
_____
_____
_____
_____
_____

3. List your core skills and areas of expertise.  Evaluate areas where you excel. What are your strengths and talents? In which areas do you consistently perform at a high level? What accomplishments or achievements demonstrate that excellence you possess? What activities have you participated in outside of formal education and work?

_____
_____
_____
_____
_____
_____

3. What are your most significant contributions in your previous roles or projects? Reflect on tasks that come naturally to you.  Which tasks or activities do you find easy to perform?  What skills do you possess that make these tasks easier for you? What positive feedback or recognition have you received for these tasks?  What skills or competencies did you gain from these activities?

_____
_____
_____
_____
_____
_____
_____

4. Identify your leadership experience and any notable achievements in leading teams.  Did you hold any leadership positions or take on significant responsibilities?

_____
_____
_____
_____
_____
_____

6. List your technical skills, software proficiencies, or specialized knowledge.  What are your strengths and talents?  In which areas do you consistently perform at a high level?  What accomplishments or achievements demonstrate your excellence?

_____
_____
_____
_____
_____
_____
_____
_____

7. Reflect on your ability to adapt to change or handle challenging situations. Describe a situation where you had to make a quick decision and what were the results. Did you ever deal with a coworker or boss who you were not seeing eye to eye on something and what did you do?

_____
_____
_____
_____

8. List any professional memberships, affiliations, or industry-related involvements.

_____
_____
_____
_____

9. Identify any additional languages you are proficient in, both written and spoken.

_____
_____

10. Reflect on your problem-solving and analytical skills.  Assess projects with remarkable results.  Recall projects or initiatives where you achieved outstanding outcomes.  What specific skills or strategies contributed to those results?  How did you overcome challenges or obstacles during those projects?

_____

_____
_____
_____
_____
_____
_____
_____
_____
_____

11. List personal references in your network. List their name, title, company, years known, relationship to you, and their contact number and email address.

_____
_____
_____
_____
_____

12. List some topics and things you are most passionate about?  How would you relate them to a specific profession or field?

| Passion | Profession/Trade |
|---------|------------------|
|         |                  |
|         |                  |
|         |                  |
|         |                  |
|         |                  |

# Appendix B: Transferable Skills Worksheet

Based on each transferable skill, list relevant work and life experiences you can mention to a prospective employer to highlight those skills.

**Communication** – Facilitated effective collaboration among team members, resulting in improved productivity and morale.

_____
_____
_____
_____
_____

**Problem-solving** – Implemented a customer feedback system, resulting in a 15% improvement in overall customer satisfaction.

_____
_____
_____
_____

**Leadership** – Managed a team of 10 sales representatives, exceeding quarterly targets by 25%.

_____
_____
_____
_____

**Teamwork** – Led a cross-functional team to successfully deliver a complex project within budget and ahead of schedule.

_____
_____
_____
_____

**Adaptability** – Adapted to a new software system and trained colleagues on its implementation, enhancing overall team efficiency.

_____
_____
_____
_____

**Critical thinking** – Quickly made a strategic decision during a crisis, mitigating potential risks and ensuring minimal disruption to operations.

_____
_____
_____

# Appendix C: Unique Selling Points-Strengths, Weaknesses and Goals

Use this sheet to document your skills and areas for improvement or further learning. Identify skills you consider strengths by marking them as "Strength" and mark areas where improvement or learning is needed as "Weakness." For skills marked as weaknesses, establish priorities for when you would like to enhance or learn them, or mark them as future goals (TBD). By completing this sheet, you will gain awareness of your strengths and areas for growth, enabling you to set goals and make improvements. Based on your priorities, you can create a learning schedule to guide your development.

| Task/Skill | Strength | Weakness | Goal Priority |
|---|---|---|---|
|  |  |  |  |
|  |  |  |  |
|  |  |  |  |
|  |  |  |  |
|  |  |  |  |
|  |  |  |  |
|  |  |  |  |
|  |  |  |  |
|  |  |  |  |
|  |  |  |  |
|  |  |  |  |
|  |  |  |  |
|  |  |  |  |
|  |  |  |  |
|  |  |  |  |
|  |  |  |  |
|  |  |  |  |
|  |  |  |  |
|  |  |  |  |
|  |  |  |  |
|  |  |  |  |
|  |  |  |  |
|  |  |  |  |
|  |  |  |  |
|  |  |  |  |

*Your strengths are your unique selling points that you want to embellish on and emphasize.

Identify and list 3-5 goals for your professional growth. These goals can be communicated to your employer as future initiatives.

_____

_____

_____

_____

_____

# Appendix D: SMART Goals Chart

Utilize this sheet to establish goals and support your commitment to follow through. The purpose of this chart is to help you stay focused, regardless of whether it leads to a successful job placement or not.

- Review job
    - Company: _____
    - Title/Position: _____
    - Contact Details: _____
    - Website: _____
    - Date Viewed: _____
- Update and tailor Resume with job description / requirements. Name file with company name.
- Update Cover Letter with job description / requirements. Name file with company name.
- Submit application.
    - Date Applied: _____
- Initial Contact from Employer
    - Date and Time: _____    Email or Phone: _____
    - Person who contacted: _____
    - Notes: _____
    _____
- Send a thank you note to the individual who contacted you.
- Next steps
    - _____
    - _____
- First (official) Interview
    - Date and Time: _____
    - Interviewer Contact information: _____
    _____
    - Notes: _____
    _____
    - Send a thank you letter to the Interviewer.
- Second Interview, if relevant.
    - Date and Time: _____
    - Interviewer Contact information: _____
    _____
    - Notes: _____
    _____
    - Send a thank you letter to the Interviewer.
- Third Interview, if relevant.
    - Date and Time: _____
    - Interviewer Contact information: _____
    _____
    - Notes: _____
    _____
    - Send a thank you letter to the Interviewer.
- Rejection or Hire Date: _____
- Send a letter to all for the opportunity to interview if not hired.
- Notes: _____

# Appendix E: Job Hunting Roadmap

Here is a guideline to get you started on the job-hunting process. A good idea is to write answers to each question for each company that you are interviewing with and tailoring your responses to the company and the position you are applying for.

**1. Research the company:**
Gain a thorough understanding of the company's mission, core values, products/services they offer, and any recent news that might be important to know. This knowledge will help you tailor your answers and demonstrate your genuine interest in the company. You might even consider reaching out to employees currently at the company through LinkedIn and see if they have any advice for you during the application process.

**2. Prepare your resume and cover letter.**
Create a resume and cover letter that shows your value to the company, highlighting skills and experiences that fit the job you are seeking. Avoid generic templates, quantify your accomplishments, and make sure it looks clean and professional. This is the first thing a prospective employer sees so put your best foot forward.

**3. Develop your elevator pitch:**
Craft a brief, engaging introduction about yourself, summarizing your background, skills, and accomplishments. This will help you confidently respond to the "Tell me about yourself" question and make a strong first impression. Remember that an elevator pitch should be short and to the point. Try to keep it under 1 minute.

**4. Prepare common interview questions:**
Anticipate common interview questions such as "Tell me about yourself," "Why are you interested in this position?" or "What are your strengths and weaknesses?" Practice concise and compelling responses that highlight your qualifications and experiences.

**5. Practice active listening:**
During the interview, focus on actively listening to the interviewer's questions and comments. This will help you provide relevant answers and build rapport with the interviewer.

**6. Use the STAR method:**
When answering behavioral or situational questions, use the STAR method (Situation, Task, Action, Result) to structure your responses. This technique helps you provide specific examples that showcase your skills and achievements.

**7. Prepare your own questions:**
Be ready to ask thoughtful questions about the company, role, team dynamics, or any other relevant topics. This demonstrates your interest and engagement in the interview process.

### 8. Practice mock interviews:

Enlist a friend or family member to conduct mock interviews with you. Simulate a real interview scenario and receive feedback on your body language, tone, and content of your answers.

### 9. Enhance non-verbal communication:

Pay attention to your body language, maintain good eye contact, sit upright, and use natural gestures. Practice conveying confidence, professionalism, and enthusiasm through your non-verbal cues.

### 10. Showcase your accomplishments:

Prepare specific examples of how you contributed to previous projects, overcame challenges, or achieved significant results. Use metrics and quantifiable achievements whenever possible to highlight your impact.

### 11. Research the interviewer:

If you know who will be conducting the interview, research their background and professional experience. This can help you establish common ground and build rapport during the conversation.

> Utilizing LinkedIn proves beneficial for researching interviewers and their respective companies. Take time to peruse their profiles to glean insights into their areas of interest and their recent activity. This approach fosters a connection with the interviewer, helping to demystify their role and making the interaction less intimidating.

### 12. Follow-up with a thank-you note:

After the interview, send a personalized thank-you email or note to express your gratitude for the opportunity and reiterate your interest in the position. This simple gesture demonstrates professionalism and leaves a positive impression.

### 13. Never Give Up:

Finding a job is a job. Don't give up at the slightest setbacks. Learn from each attempt and improve on the process, even if it's only a little thing at a time. Your dream job is out there waiting for you to land it.

# Ronald Demitris

**Address**: 123 McClay Drive, Houston, TX, 73301, United States
**Email**: rdemitris@gmail.com
**Mobile**: (555) 259-1212
**LinkedIn**: https://www.linkedin.com/in/ronalddemitris/

---

Software Developer with 7+ years of experience software design, development, system integration, testing and release process as well as the management of projects, budgets and personnel to ensure project completion in a timely manner.

## Professional Experience

**Senior Programmer Analyst**, Chase, Houston, TX                    *From August 2020 to Present*

- Migrating legacy systems to VMWare within allotted budget; Managing Dell host server and all upgrades.
- Migrating legacy Windows servers to newer Windows 2016/2019 Server, SQL 2017/2019 DB servers.
- Implement a CI/CD process to help get smaller changes in shorter time to production and with fewer bugs using Agile concepts.
- Developed Web Front End and Mobile version using wireframes, main website analysis and prioritizing functional elements to provide the customer a better experience. (SASS/Scripting)

**Programmer I**, Santander., New Orleans, LA                    *From July 2016 to August 2020*

- Elicit requirements, analyze impact on end users, create UI mock-ups, develop, test, and document all functional requirements for application used to control service access on the department floor.
- Developed a multi-tiered, multi-threaded Java application to read and write data to a database via command line arguments as well as direct JDBC access to tables depending on available technology.
- Designed and developed PDF reports to dynamically pull data from the database using PDF library SDK.

## Education

**Louisiana State University**
Baton Rouge, LA, United States
*2010 - 2014*
Bachelor of Science, Finance

## Additional Skills

-Proficient in MS Office (Word, Excel, PowerPoint, Outlook)
-Salesforce
- C#
- Java
- SQL
-TFS Project Management
-Fluent in English, Spanish, and French

# Appendix G: Sample Functional Resume

The following type of resume highlights your skills in a functional format. It also shows how you can add work hours per week to meet some government requirements for a resume.

---

# Jane Smith

• (212) 555-1212 • jsmith114@test.com

Drawing on three decades of advancing expertise in software design, development, system integration, migration, testing, and release processes, I possess a wealth of technical and managerial acumen. As a detail-oriented and results-driven Manager, I prioritize effective leadership and communication to execute projects of diverse scopes, adhering to budgetary and resource constraints. My proficiency extends to incorporating cutting-edge technologies and emphasizing security measures in all endeavors.

---

### Technical Skills

C#  API/Web Services     Source Safe/TFS  DHCP/DNS/AD/DMZ  VMWare  IIS  SharePoint WIKI
Windows Servers   Excel   Word  Photoshop JIRA/Trello/Teams   SQL
Documentation: Functional Specs, Design Specs, SIT/SAT, UAT, Developer Test Cases
Currently working on Scrum Master Certification.

---

| Education | **Adelphi**, NY | **BA Computer Science- Magna Cum Laude**, 2000 |
|---|---|---|
| | **SUNY, Rochester**, NY | **MS Computer Science**, 2004 |

---

### Professional Summary

#### *Management and Leadership*

- Managed IT personnel, both local and remote, overseeing the development and maintenance of a variety of legacy and new applications and infrastructure needs within defined constraints, budget, and security requirements.
- Conducted hiring, performance reviews, professional development, conflict resolutions and on occasion managed termination decisions for Development and IT teams.
- Research and propose changes and enhancements to Executive team and departments for new equipment and security options to enhance growth and efficiency and speed up time to delivery of client's products.
- Fostered a culture of collaboration, continuous growth and knowledge sharing among departments, promoting interdepartmental knowledge exchange, communication, conflict resolutions and working to build unified teams.

#### *Project Management*

- Provided the necessary updates, documentation, and provisions to apply for and maintain PCI compliance with Visa and Wells Fargo for safe and secure credit card processing applications.
- Onboard new clients during company merger and supporting the integration of existing applications with new systems.
- Developed real-time articles and information on the advertising world's current trends and news on the Agency's in-house web blog.
- Elicit requirements, analyze impact on end users, create UI mock-ups, develop, test and document all functional requirements.

- Initiated development of QA discipline within Agency to provide a better and well-coordinated testing environment for client projects and providing for a better test and release environment, providing testing and UAT documentation.

*Infrastructure, Network Management, and Operations*
- Migrated existing applications and systems onto new infrastructure to provide a smooth transition during merger.
- Managed 22 facilities, providing real-time 24/7 support including procurement of facility equipment and software, managing licenses, vendors, and third-party services to provide higher and consistent delivery for client products.
- Managed the servicing of IT troubleshooting tickets, ensuring 98% or better throughput for all 22 facilities, 6 data centers and 2 headquarters with up to 625-850 end users, season based.
- Managed bicoastal EDI Retail departments working with TieKinetics, SPS, CommerceHub, and manual EDI files.
- Provided after-hours support for facilities during power outages and during a data center failure.
- Provided critical systems maintenance and support during 9/11 crisis at TRU.
- Updated internal IT policies to meet current and future demands and implement companywide security standards.

*Application Design, Development, Testing and Release*
- Led the design, development, and testing of web and standalone applications including product analysis, development, testing, and client interaction to build efficient and streamlined systems with timely deliverables (REST/C#/VB.net/VB/PHP/ColdFusion/ASP/SQL/Access).
- Database Management for SQL, MySQL, and Access DB.
- Collaborated with business analysts, product managers, and clients to elicit requirements, analyze system changes' impact, and ensure all functional requirements were incorporated into the final design and specification documents, following Agile concepts.
- Worked with developers to improve manual testing skills and emphasize the importance of quality assurance throughout the development lifecycle.
- Participated in SDLC standardization for CMM Level 1 and 2, creating the required documentation for each project, including System Integration Testing and System Acceptance Testing, Functional Specs

Work Experience

| | |
|---|---|
| **ABC,** Houston, TX, **IT Director, Operations**, 55-60 h/w | 9/2014 – 6/2022 |
| **DLG,** Santa Barbara, CA, **Sr. Web Developer**, 40 h/w | 7/2013 – 6/2014 |
| **HiEnd**, Torrance, CA, **Senior Developer**, 40-50 h/w | 5/2007 – 6/2013 |
| **TRU**, Rochester, NY, **Sr. Programmer Analyst**, 50-60 h/w | 1/2004 – 4/2007 |
| **KGI**, Brooklyn, NY, **Programmer II**, 40-50 h/w | 1/2000 – 1/2004 |

Personal Projects – Making a Difference Outside the Technical Realm          Ongoing
Chief Editor for The Journal of all Life Events
Voting Board Member-Secretary for Sciences Academy

# Appendix H: Sample Cover Letter

I am writing to express my strong interest in the position of Director of Software Engineering at ITL. With over 30 years of experience in IT and Operations, project management, infrastructure, network management, and application design and development, I am confident in my ability to contribute to your organization's success.

In my previous role as IT Director, I successfully managed diverse teams of IT professionals, overseeing the development and maintenance of various applications and infrastructure while adhering to defined constraints, budgets, and security requirements. I also led the Helpdesk Support Team, achieving a 98% or better throughput and execution of troubleshooting tickets across 7 facilities, 2 data centers, and 2 separate headquarters. This real-time 24/7 support, coupled with efficient procurement of equipment, software, and third-party services, resulted in enhanced delivery of client products. Additionally, I maintained the infrastructure of various devices, such as servers, networks, desktops, scanners, tablets, and printers across multiple facilities, prioritizing secure inter-device communication and data integrity.

Additionally, I have navigated through 2 mergers, created comprehensive roadmaps to unify various applications, networking, and infrastructure needs into one framework, exceeding future growth and productivity goals while mitigating risks and maximizing resource utilization.

My expertise in infrastructure and network management has enabled me to seamlessly migrate applications and systems, maintain secure inter-device communication, diagnose, and troubleshoot server and network issues, and plan and coordinate physical relocations of IT labs. I have also managed the IT infrastructure for multiple facilities, ensuring the smooth operation of servers, networks, desktops, scanners, tablets, and printers while prioritizing secure inter-device communication and data integrity.

Furthermore, I have led the design, development, testing, and release of web applications, prioritizing user experience and collaborating with stakeholders to ensure all functional specifications are met. With an extensive background in technologies such as ASP.NET, C#, VB, C++, Java, SQL, PHP, ColdFusion, and COBOL, I possess the skills to analyze problems and find viable solutions at all levels. I am always eager to learn and stay updated with emerging technologies.

With a detail-oriented and hardworking approach, I take pride in delivering quality work and never shying away from a challenge. My ability to mentor team members, interact with clients and stakeholders, and manage budgets and schedules adds value to my leadership capabilities.

I am confident that my skills and experiences align perfectly with the requirements of the position. I am eager to contribute my expertise and drive success within your organization. I am extremely detail oriented, hardworking, and dependable. I believe in taking pride of ownership in everything that I do and never turn away from a challenge without, at least, trying to find a viable solution.

Thank you for considering my application, and I look forward to the opportunity to discuss how I can contribute to your team.

Feel free to contact me at 212.555.1212, or jsmith114@test.com.

Sincerely,
Jane Smith

# Appendix I: Sample Email for Networking in LinkedIn

You should customize the email to align with your specific goals and the individual you are reaching out to. Personalization and genuine interest are key to making a positive impression and increasing the likelihood of a response.

---

Subject: Introduction and Request for Insights

Dear [Contact's Name],

I hope this email finds you well. My name is [Your Name], and I recently came across your profile on LinkedIn. I was impressed by your extensive experience and achievements in the marketing field, particularly in [specific area of interest or expertise].

As someone who is passionate about marketing and aspiring to transition into a similar role, I would greatly appreciate the opportunity to learn from your experiences and gain insights into the industry. Your expertise and career journey are truly inspiring, and I believe I can benefit greatly from your wisdom.

If you are available, I would be grateful for a brief conversation at your convenience. I understand your time is valuable, so I suggest a 15–20-minute call where we can discuss your experiences, challenges faced, and any advice you may have for someone looking to enter this field. I am flexible and can accommodate a time that works best for you, or I am also open to chatting in text. Please let me know your availability, and I will adjust accordingly.

Thank you for considering my request. I understand that you are busy, and I genuinely appreciate any time you can spare for this conversation. I look forward to the possibility of connecting with and learning from you.

Best regards,

[Your Name]
[Your Contact Information]

# Appendix J: Sample Professional Review for a Colleague

The following is an example of a professional review for a software developer. You can use a similar format for other professions and highlight the individuals' strengths and skills.

[Colleague's Name] is an exceptional software developer who has made a significant impact within our team. Their technical expertise, problem-solving skills, and commitment to delivering high-quality code are truly commendable. I have had the pleasure of working closely with [Colleague's Name] on various projects, and I am consistently impressed by their ability to tackle complex challenges with ease and precision.

One of the standout qualities of [Colleague's Name] is their strong attention to detail. They consistently produce clean, efficient, and reliable code, contributing to the overall success of our projects. Their ability to analyze problems and develop innovative solutions sets them apart as a top-notch developer.

In addition to their technical skills, [Colleague's Name] is a great team player. They actively contribute to group discussions, sharing insights and suggestions that enhance collaboration and lead to more efficient workflows. Their positive attitude and willingness to assist others are truly appreciated by the entire team.

I have also witnessed [Colleague's Name] adapt quickly to changing project requirements and embrace new technologies. They are always eager to expand their skill set and stay updated with the latest industry trends. Their commitment to continuous learning is inspiring and ensures they are at the forefront of their field.

Overall, [Colleague's Name] is a highly skilled software developer who consistently delivers outstanding results. Their dedication, technical prowess, and collaborative mindset make them an invaluable asset to any organization. I highly recommend [Colleague's Name] to any team or project seeking a talented and driven software developer.

Feel free to connect with [Colleague's Name] on LinkedIn to learn more about their impressive portfolio and experience.

# Appendix K: GEMS

Here are some gems you can take with you as you pursue your career goals.

- Standing out from the crowd is essential. (p8)
- Transferable skills are versatile abilities that can be applied to various roles and industries. (p12)
- Delve into your strengths (p13)
- Passions are the fuel that ignites a person's drive and enthusiasm. (p14)
- Unique selling points (USPs) - These are the qualities and attributes that differentiate you from other candidates. (p15)
- Your personal brand is the image and reputation you cultivate in the professional world. (p17)
- Your Portfolio - It serves as a dynamic representation of your accomplishments and expertise. (p20)
- Your elevator pitch will need to highlight your key skills, experiences, and accomplishments, while showcasing your adaptability, leadership abilities, and technical prowess in a few short sentences. (p25)
- Finding that sliver of time [to set goals and continue learning] can become a pivotal step toward achieving your professional aspirations. (p28)
- Having a clear direction will help guide your job search efforts and narrow down your efforts to meaningful searches. (p30)
- A job search can take time, so remain persistent, proactive, and open to opportunities. (p36)
- Networking - It is a strategic investment that can significantly propel your career forward and open doors to new possibilities. (p38)
- Your personal brand is a reflection of your professional identity. (p44)
- By focusing on relationship-building rather than transactional interactions, you cultivate a network that is genuinely invested in your success. (p45)
- A strong professional online presence will showcase you as a prospective candidate to a future employer. (p48)
- Use the summary section in your resume to draw attention to your main qualifications. (p59)
- Attention to detail is paramount when it comes to your resume. (p65)
- It's important to know what audience you are applying to when writing your cover letter. (p69)
- Learn how to align your skills and experiences with the job requirements. (p73)
- The difference between landing a job and being passed over could depend on your own inquisitiveness. (p75)
- Using the STAR method, your answers become more structured, focused, and impactful, allowing you to effectively demonstrate your skills and experiences to potential employers. (p78)
- A well-crafted follow-up message or thank-you note can leave a lasting impression and set you apart from other candidates (p82)
- Building a fulfilling and prosperous career requires continuous growth, adaptability, and a proactive mindset (p83)
- Never let failure be an option. (p86)

- The ability to effectively convey your ideas transcends language fluency and is a valuable asset in any career. (p87)
- Leadership skills are versatile assets that benefit individuals across all career stages and roles (p87)
- The quest for knowledge and skill development knows no bounds and can be pursued at any stage of life. (p88)
- The path to one's career ambitions often presents obstacles and moments of stress, so it's crucial to prioritize the well-being of your mind, body, and emotions along the way. (p93)

www.ingramcontent.com/pod-product-compliance
Lightning Source LLC
Chambersburg PA
CBHW072326290526
45794CB00002B/752